The Great Escape from Nihilism

Rediscovering Our Passion in Late Modernity

Gordon E. Carkner, PhD

The Great Escape from Nihilism

Published in Canada by Infocus Publishing
3731 Millar Court
Abbotsford, BC V2S 7K5

ISBN 978-0-9950968-2-0

To Ute, Kierianne and Hannah

We also want to dedicate this work to two phenomenal people who have been a great encouragement to the author over several years: recently deceased Professor John Webster of St. Andrew's University, the author's PhD supervisor, whose tireless patience and finely nuanced insights helped to guide and shape his thinking about faith and culture in late modernity; and recently deceased Dr. Philip Hill, faculty member of Mechanical Engineering at the University of British Columbia and formerly of Queen's University, Kingston, Ontario. Both were generous souls who offered wise mentorship and inspiration; both raised the bar of academic and personal character excellence.

About the Author

Gordon Carkner is a visionary, passionate about dialogue on salient questions of meaning and identity, faith and culture. He has worked as a meta-educator, a networker, and campus pastor for over 30 years in Canadian universities. As a voracious reader, his vision is to mentor future leaders within academia with excellent resources: to keep them on the cutting edge and to broaden their horizons. Together with his team of university faculty and graduate students, he has sponsored countless book studies, lectures, panels, discussions and debates on the connection between a wide range of academic scholarship and Christian faith, helping people find their voice, grow their identity, and develop a spirit of curiosity. His present work is located in Vancouver, Canada at the University of British Columbia. He is also keen to feed relevant scholarship intelligence and critical thinking insights to church leaders. He is joined in his work by his lovely wife and ministry partner Ute and their two charming daughters. As a family, they enjoy getting out in the mountains of British Columbia, Alberta, and the Austrian and Swiss Alps. Gordon and Ute together have hiked the Grand Canyon and Ute joined an Australian expedition in Nepal.

Dr. Carkner holds a B.Sc. in Human Physiology from Queen's University in Kingston, Ontario, Canada; a Masters of Divinity from Trinity Evangelical Divinity School in Deerfield, Illinois; and a PhD in philosophical theology from University of Wales, with a strong emphasis on the moral self and the making of the modern identity. His curiosity and expertise lies in the arena of questions concerning freedom and the good, secularity, meaning, worldviews, and philosophical anthropology, as they get articulated, discussed and debated within late modern Western culture. His current intellectual hero is Canadian McGill University philosopher, Professor Emeritus Charles Taylor. He is also well read in history and philosophy of science, science and theology. Gordon co-authored with Michael Green the popular book *Ten Myths about Christianity,* which sold over 200,000 copies in twenty languages and assisted many people around the world to reconsider what faith offers to their journey in life. He has also authored a number of key papers on scientism, individualism, worldviews and pluralism, tools for effective dialogue, and Charles Taylor's recovery of the good for moral discourse. He hosts an active blog for postgraduate students, which reaches people in 92 countries, at www.ubcgcu.org.

Table of Contents

Acknowledgments

One never operates alone, and thus there are numerous people that we want to appreciate for their input and advice on this project. Professor John Webster then of Christ Church, Oxford and Dr. Donn Welton of Stony Brook University in New York, as first and second readers respectively, offered wise direction of the research for the 2006 doctoral dissertation: *A Critical Examination of Michel Foucault's Concept of Moral Self-Constitution in Dialogue with Charles Taylor*. This discussion grounds the journey of the book. Much appreciation also goes out to the scholars and graduate students at the Oxford Center for Mission Studies and the University of Wales who tested the fecundity of many of the concepts as they were being formulated. IVCF in British Columbia, under the direction of Neil Graham, was generous to allow a sabbatical year to start the PhD research. We also appreciate dialogue with serious thinkers in IFES.

Over the years, the writer has had the privilege to know and engage with many faculty members at Universities of Guelph, Waterloo, Laurier and University of British Columbia, Simon Fraser University, Regent College, University of the Fraser Valley and Trinity Western University. They are too many to name all, but certain faculty interlocutors stand out in one's memory as inspiring examples, sound but creative thinkers, scholars and scientists: Dr. John North, Dr. David Matthews, Dr. Philip Hill, Dr. Olav Slaymaker, Dr. Judith Toronchuk, Dr. David Ley, Dr. Dennis Danielson, Dr. Martin Barlow, Dr. George Egerton, Dr. John Redekop, Dr. Craig Mitton, Dr. Ed Piers, Dr. Bert Cameron, Dr. Bart vander Kamp, Dr. John Owen, Dr. James Sire (former IVP editor), Dr. Arnold Sikkemma, Professor Ron Dart, Dr. Barry Pointon, Dr. Martin Ester and Dr. Tim Huh. All have been exemplary in taking seriously both their faith and scholarship; they have shown passion in their teaching and a deep respect for students. The discourse of the book indicates that a wealth of authors helped to shape the writer's mind and heart, giving life rich meaning and offering inspiration. All these mentors and their diligent work are much appreciated. The book is part of a larger group thought project, tapping into a fine community of scholars and public intellectuals.

In terms of high caliber dialogue on non-religious campuses, great inspiration has been taken from the Pascal Lectures at University of Waterloo, the Faraday Institute of Science and Religion at Cambridge University, BioLogos in the USA, the Canadian Science and Christian Affiliation, Christians in Science in the UK, the American Scientific Affiliation, the Gifford Lectures in Edinburgh, and the work of the Veritas Forum, which began at Harvard University. The UBC Graduate and Faculty Christian Forum, over some twenty-five plus years, has empowered cross-disciplinary discussion on a wide variety of topics, integrating faith and academic learning. We are grateful for the numerous top international scholars and scientists who contributed to this series beginning with Sir John Plolkinghorne of Queens' College, Cambridge. Many of the faculty mentioned above helped to shape this series and have offered thoughtful and inspiring presentations.

Credit must be attributed to the many bright students who have been a part of our lives and community. Their passion for excellence and energy for making a strong contribution to the common good is nothing short of inspirational. They helped to formulate and test ideas, push the envelope, at Universities of Guelph, Waterloo, Sir Wilfrid Laurier and University of British Columbia, but also at conferences in Europe and North America. We value their intense curiosity, critical thinking skill and vision. Thanks go out to all followers of the Graduate Christian Union blog (www.ubcgcu.org), whose feedback has been invaluable to the production of this volume.

Friends who have been willing to read and help edit this manuscript at various stages are: Olav Slaymaker, Tim Dickau, Ron

Dart, Barry Pointon, Matthew Larsen, Bethany Murphy and Jan Porcino.

Our colleague at Outreach Canada, Cam Taylor, with much patience and diligence helped with the layout and final presentation, and the whole OC team have been very supportive, including Craig Kraft the Executive Director and his team. We are very grateful for their servant leadership.

Finally, I want to recognize the tremendous support of my family, my wife Ute and my two wonderful, creative daughters Kierianne and Hannah. Kierianne read and gave astute feedback on the text as a young assistant editor.

Preface

This book is about a journey out of nihilism into the heart of meaning. Late modernity is a characterization of today's highly developed, global societies in continuity with modernity, but more complex and conflicted. This era is also characterized by rapid social change, a disembedding of self from local contexts, from history, with a loss of tradition—a period of globalization. The individual has become the new center of agency. Identity is an *auto-biographical* project, something we actively construct rather than receive from ancestors or village of origin. These are challenging and adventurous times.

The journey begins by raising a key question: Does nihilism have the last word? The following discussion addresses a crisis of faith, a crisis of identity, a sense of *lostness* in late modernity. The journey operates in three phases: a. Analysis of the Problem or Crisis of Nihilism (Part 1 and Part 2, Chapters 1 to 5); b. Hope of a Recovery on the Horizon (Part 2, Chapters 6-8); and c. Proposal for of an Alternative Vision for a Way Forward (Part 2, Chapters 9 and 10). Nihilism is characterized by the *absolute status of the will*. Our companions on the journey are a fine, seasoned group of writers, poets, philosophers, social reformers, psychiatrists, scientists, theologians, among other scholars and public intellectuals. These are key people who have made their mark, shaped the public mind and continue to impact Western culture and global cultures. They are people who dig deep and bring substantial answers to the dilemma of our time.

The Great Escape from Nihilism is about a courageous and somewhat dangerous journey, but ultimately a path towards hopeful alternatives to the forces that weigh down our spirits and the tensions that divide us. Is living in our current prison camp of nihilism any kind of reasonable option? We must decide in our minds and our hearts that the quest to escape is worth the risks. The ten conversations are modeled on real, ongoing discussions and debates over several years on university campuses across Canada, America, Britain and Continental Europe. There is a feeling of urgency in them. Universities are still some of the most discursive environments in our culture, where the pursuit of insight into truth and the search for innovative answers to problems is encouraged. They are also intense identity shaping crucibles. Through the span of these conversations, we want to reveal the art of effective dialogue. We contend that, despite their practical value, there is more to life than science, technology, business and algorithms. Our journey involves the quest for the Holy Grail of human flourishing, the deeper life, the *thick* self.

The Crisis

The journey begins with an identification of what we mean by nihilism and how it obscures our vision. We are confronting a most powerful cultural myth of naked, amoral choice and radical autonomy in nihilism. It includes our infatuation with the promise of limitless freedom. After this, it leans into the winds of complex ideas like the good, the ideology of the aesthetic, love, humanism and meaning. Like in the epic 1963 film *The Great Escape*, much thought, planning and excavation is involved in the quest for negotiating our cultural context in late modernity. We begin with an identification of the sources and character of nihilism in Part 1. We want to tunnel through some of the divisive attitudes that fill us with anxiety: anger, cynicism, hatred and bigotry, isolation of self, confusion about morality, fear of and contempt for others.

We also want to challenge the hegemony of certain ideologies or worldviews: scientism, materialism, aestheticism, rationalism, the view that science has replaced religion, and popular conceptions of secularism. It will require some healthy skepticism concerning reigning cultural assumptions. Evil and suffering arise as a key issue that affronts all our sensibilities, and we discover to our shock that nihilism abandons us in our pain. Finally, under the crisis, we want to interact with a late modern attempt to recover from nihilism, the aesthetic self of famous Parisian philosopher Michel Foucault. Does he succeed in his attempt to escape? The book remains invested in the life of critical reflection, as well as hopeful suggestions for ongoing and sustainable transformation—new ways forward. Nihilism, hard rationalism and philosophical materialism have come under serious challenge and scrutiny in our day, both as an adequate explanatory paradigm and source of creativity. We need better interpretive schemes, better maps, to make sense of human society, ways that fit the facts, bring us together, and improve our relationships.

Hopeful Horizons for a Recovery of Culture

Why should we settle for narrow, often mindless, culture wars and tribalism? We begin the journey as an escape from the grip of cultural, social and personal nihilism. We end with a serious proposition for a paradigm shift in thinking, a way to think differently about the world, and our place in it. Charles Taylor, our principle investigative philosopher in the escape, calls this our *social imaginary*. But we need a *hinge* or bridge to prepare us for that new vision. In order to break free from the stranglehold of nihilism, we must explore and recover richer uses of language such as the good and *agape* love. It is part of a recovery project, because these are ancient concepts that can inspire and power our imagination once again. For many, the journey may seem difficult, like boring through a mountain in Switzerland, with much grinding, dirt and darkness before one sees glimpses of the light. It involves a steady commitment to think and compare notes—true reflective grit.

After the stage is set for dialogue about our context within the immanent frame in Part 1 and Part 2, Chapters 1 to 5, we start to explore other ways of seeing. We move towards a vision of a larger horizon and a greater context for our identity and purpose. It involves real grappling about what is important for our mutual survival in the twenty-first century crucible of time. A wager is made on transcendence of the moral good and *agape* love—a philosophical *turn*. This turn offers perspective and tools to deal with some of today's vexing problems, as well as re-constituting moral agency. New ideas, horizons of opportunity, mutuality, understanding and human flourishing emerge before our eyes. New, insightful interlocutors are invited to the table because we need fresh eyes to think differently about our future.

Actualization of the New Vision

Now the question remains, can it be lived practically? What is the ultimate traction of this vision of a brave new world? While facing reality at all costs, we want to take a new position, a new posture towards others and the world. The involves recovery of moral agency and fresh motivation now that we have escaped the confines of nihilism. As we cross the open fields outside the camp, we need a compass to navigate new freedom and a map that has useful content. It is a very exciting adventure indeed, one where we explore the transcendent turn towards incarnational humanism. For it is in the incarnation of Jesus Christ that we catch a glimpse of the light of deeper freedom, of a whole new plausibility structure for life.

Although it does not attempt to be comprehensive, the discussion offers a solid trajectory: towards fruitful lives of mutual understanding and faithful presence. It takes other persons seriously as potential collaborators to live out *agape* love and commit to the common good. The goal of this new humanism is greater flourishing of the whole person and the whole of society: Global South as well as Global North. Welcome to this gripping adventure of rethinking who we are, where we are located, and how we might navigate the landscape of late modernity. Our reflection on these matters is urgent and consequential to our very survival. We trust that it will help you discover wisdom, make a personal breakthrough and locate your passion in our complex age.

PART 1

The Problem We Face

Introduction

In this discussion, we want to engage the ideology of nihilism. It has taken many captive. Some are passive participants while others are self-consciously involved and have become active promoters. Nihilism is related to how we approach the world, how we choose and how we perceive *reality*. The interrogation of this outlook promotes dialogue about some crucial issues in late modernity, our current situation at this stage of Western Enlightenment. Working diligently together to decipher the code, we will expose the ideology to critical examination, and we anticipate some pertinent discoveries. We have chosen Charles Taylor as our principle investigative assistant. As one of the great thinkers of our time, he will be of great help to move our discussion onto significantly higher ground. He is one of the top twelve living philosophers, the preeminent Canadian philosopher in the political, cultural and moral realm, and the premiere philosopher of Western modernity. With his help, we hope that through discerning our location within Western culture, we can explore the claim that *nihilism does not have the last word*.

What follows is a deep structure protest that there are broader horizons and layers of meaning to be explored, researched and discovered. The journey ahead entails an archival rediscovery of lost language, lost potential in relationships, lost perspective on our lives. The discussion proceeds as a committed liberation project, because many today long to escape the confines, addictions and seductions of nihilism. The project is both a cultural probe and a quest. In his landmark book *A Secular Age* (2007), Taylor offers a monumental analysis of our philosophical and cultural climate, explaining how we have gotten here and where we might be headed. The stakes are high. He traces how we moved from theism through deism to atheism over 500 years, during roughly 1500 to 2000 C.E. But in this substantial, prize-winning tome, he also explores how we can rethink and refresh the current debate about our identity and the nature of our 'secularity'. Who indeed are we late moderns? What are the possibilities for dialogue between people of such divergent philosophical and ethical positions? How can we live and work together in a positive way? What are the interpretive keys for unlocking the mystery of our age, its spiritual and cultural imagination? Taylor claims:

> Our language has lost, and needs to have restored, its constitutive power. This means that we can deal instrumentally with realities around us but their deeper meaning (the background in which they exist) the higher reality which finds expression in them, is ignored and often invisible to us. Our language has lost the power to *Name* things in their embedding, their deeper, richer and higher reality. The current incapacity of language is a crucial factor in our incapacity of *seeing well* and flourishing. Our language, our vision and our lives often remain flattened in late modernity. (C. Taylor, 2007, 761)

The discussion that follows is an attempt to recover the richness of language and also the larger horizon of its meaning. In both *A Secular Age* (2007) and his prior landmark discussion on philosophical anthropology, *Sources of the Self* (1989), Taylor documents a major change in the *social imaginary*. That entails its interpretive background, or way things seem to make sense to us. One might also refer to it as the conditions of plausibility. There has been a shift in *ethos,* one that includes people's basic sensibilities, their intimate assumptions and perceptions about reality. He strongly encourages us to learn from our historical roots: "Our past is sedimented in our present and we are doomed to misidentify ourselves as long as we cannot do justice to where we came from." (C. Taylor, 2007, 29). Our philosophical narrative is vital to our present self-understanding and problem-solving capacity.

Taylor notes that *human flourishing* has become our main focus of life in a period of *unbelief* in the transcendent or the divine. We have moved from a transcendent to an immanent worldview since medieval times. In the West, God was once the ultimate good for the majority of citizens, and now human flourishing is the dominant good within what he refers to as the "immanent frame" or personal horizon. Every person and every society inescapably lives by some conception of human flourishing (fulfilled life, one worth living, one which we naturally admire). It is often inscribed in ancient moral codes, philosophical theories, or religious practices and devotion. So the definition and parameters of human flourishing encompasses yet another key concept in our quest to discern our age.

Contrary to many, Taylor does not believe in the demise of religion in our post-secular age, but instead claims that we are in pursuit of more, rather than less, spirituality today. This reveals what he calls the 'Nova Effect' of multiple spiritual journeys or searches for meaning. We have not given up on spirituality and meaning; late moderns are looking for it everywhere. They are bent on making sense of their existence, even in this age of nihilism. He also speaks of *multiple modernities*, because we actually experience modernity differently in different contexts and different tribes. We are *cross-pressured*. Perhaps this is why some authors like Walter Truett Anderson (1997) speak of people employing multiple selves as a coping mechanism, one for each environment. Late moderns are definitely on a search and no one is quite sure where it will end. Perhaps the very popular Academy Award winning film *The Life of Pi* is a sample of the complexity and uncertainty of such a journey. The main character explores several religious and secular views to make sense of his adventure and there are indeed many tensions between these viewpoints. He is quite conflicted as he tries to survive, like many people today. The film's cult popularity shows significant cultural resonance with the ambivalence in the story.

Taylor notes three major forms of spirituality or 'hypergood': exclusive (scientific) humanism, which is also seen as scientism; Christian or theistic humanism; and neo-Nietzschean anti-humanism with its emphasis on exploring the full range of Dionysian appetites and desires, including cruelty. Some people also want to remake the human, or invent the human through various forms of manipulations (for example, genetic and technological manipulation). This is called *trans-humanism*. Taylor focuses attention on the first three, feeling that this tri-partite discussion is where we can find the greatest increase in understanding of our twenty-first century identity. The three visions are vital for the big picture discernment of the age we inhabit.

Western modernities are the fruit of new inventions, new stories, newly constructed self-understandings and related practices. They cannot be explained in terms of perennial features of human life. Some nominalists like Michel Foucault want nothing to do with anything essentialist called human nature *per se*. They are rooted in new forms of consciousness, a new sense of self and a whole new world picture or outlook. The following ten articles, which include ten moves, explore some of the important contours of this late modern consciousness. Perhaps you the reader will discover, amidst the critique of nihilism, a trajectory of retrieval of good things repressed (some buried for centuries), things that are deeply relevant to our present and future. But first, we must understand some key components of nihilism: the immanent frame, scientism, two distinct ways of seeing reality, and ethical relativism. By mapping the terrain of our prison and beginning with the content, we can perhaps find a way out of its existential grip. See the reaction when you inject this story of recovery into your discussion in the local pub or late night dorm discussion, or your Areopagus, where ideas get debated.

1

The Immanent Frame

In Charles Taylor, we are offered a particularly insightful analysis of our cultural *ethos*. He captures the way in which we have located ourselves in the late modern world and the picture that has taken our minds captive, shaped our mind's eye. He identifies it as the *immanent frame*. This house of the mind and imagination constitutes a unique social imaginary (implicit understanding of the space in which we live) in human history. Our focus at this point of the discussion will be to exposit the key insights of Chapter 15 in *A Secular Age* (2007) called "The Immanent Frame". In this analysis, he shows how religion has been philosophically and culturally marginalized in the West, even while it is in resurgence by numbers, especially in Latin America, Africa and Asia. Whether we do or do not value it, it is the Christian religion that has had the greatest shaping influence on western culture by many reputable accounts. As a plausibility structure, it has become marginalized, and is often barely tolerated and sometimes it is despised. One often notices a hegemony against religion within academic circles, for example. Taylor gives us tough insights and leads us to think freshly and circumspectly about how we have arrived at this cultural space, and about the nature of our current and future options.

The core theme of the book (C. Taylor, 2007, p. 510) is to study the fate of religious faith in the *strong* sense in the West, meaning: a. belief in a transcendent reality, and b. the connected aspiration of personal transformation, which goes beyond, is greater than, ordinary human flourishing. Taylor calls into question the subtraction story or Western Master Narrative (one deeply embedded in our modern consciousness), where science replaces religion after the breakup of Christendom. Within this faulty perspective, the growth of science entails the death of God and the recession of religion. In this case, religion is 'seen to be' replaced by science. Taylor asks some tough questions: Is this hermeneutically valid? When did science become equivalent to secularism and why? Where is the logic in this move? He reads this as a situation of fundamental contestability. Taylor calls into question this misperception of our western history and our current reality, suggesting that it is wanting as a hermeneutical grid (interpretive schema). For example, top scholar Mark Taylor of Columbia University notes in his 2007 book *After God*, that Western secularity is also a religious phenomenon in and of itself. For him, religion is not a separate domain but instead pervades all culture and has an important impact on every aspect of society. The simplistic notion that science has replaced religion, however popular, is extremely naïve.

In the face of this theory (subtraction story or secularity 2), Charles Taylor explores with reflective folks the plausibility of the life-nurturing, transcendent dimensions of human culture. He does not believe that all citizens of late modernity need to deny the possibility of the transcendent from within this immanent frame. They need not live within a horizontal dimension only, which includes a flattened (*thin*) form of language. From his perspective, the story of the rise of modern social spaces doesn't need to be given an anti-religious spin (C. Taylor, 2007, 579). The actual reality of Western culture is closer to the truth that "a whole gamut of positions, from the most militant atheism to the most orthodox traditional theisms, passing through every possible position on the way, are represented and defended somewhere in our society" (C. Taylor, 2007, 556). They are defended in various non-neutral contexts, institutions and communities. The actual situation is much more complex.

This actuality creates for citizens of late modernity the sense of being cross-pressured by the different views (the plurality of positions) they encounter, making them uncomfortable at times with the tension. Citizens may indeed experience these different views in different spheres of their lives. Nevertheless, plurality has a way of teaching us and making us humble about our position. The dialogue and debate of these perceptions is still very robust, with endless potential options to find meaning. Both belief and unbelief in God co-exist within society (Taylor's secularity 3 position). He articulates a more inclusive and complex reading of late modernity than we often hear from other scholars.

So what does Taylor mean by the term immanent frame? The buffered identity (as opposed to the porous pre-modern self) is a key part of such a mental frame. It operates within a disenchanted world where supernatural beings or forces with teleological goals or intentions are deemed close to impossible (C. Taylor, 2007, 539). Final causes or teleology are eliminated from one's world picture. With this immanent frame, there is a loss of a cosmic order. Everything important is this-worldly, explicable on its own terms; it fits within the time-space-energy-matter dimensions of a strictly material world. Social and political orders are constructed by humans solely for mutual benefit, not to please, or resist, a divine entity or conform to a transcendent good. Society is instead made up of atomistic individuals, who collaborate as they see fit out of mutual self-interest. Each human is charged with finding her or his own way of being human, his or her own individual spiritual path, chosen or constructed from the options available within the Nova Effect phenomenon of multiple spiritualities. Everyone has become their own measure of the good (*auto-nomos*). Consequently, their freedom to choose is a matter of primary concern, and they are ready to fight for the inviolable liberty of personal volition.

Nonetheless, the immanent frame perspective on reality is by no means ethically neutral or strictly objective. It includes some things (values such as secular time) and excludes others – it renders 'vertical' or 'transcendent' worlds as inaccessible or unthinkable, at the very least irrelevant to serious thought and life. It takes a hard moral position, and as we will see in the next section, it operates as a philosophically reductionist stance. The world is a leaner, smaller, less rich and dimensional space. Next we look at scientism as a subsidiary ideology that promotes nihilism.

2

Five Cultural Identifiers of Scientism

Scientism (and the philosophical positivism of A. J. Ayer) has been discredited by many philosophers and scientists in the twentieth century. Yet this *ideology* still seems to dominate much popular thinking, even within academia. It is particularly strong among the New Atheists, the cause of much confusion, rage and prejudice. In order for a belief to be considered valid or credible, scientism requires that it be *scientifically testable*. Thus, much claim to knowledge, even within the university, is devalued, discredited or excluded. We are required to be skeptical even about things that we know to be true by common sense means.

A valid, while limited, approach to knowing (science) somehow morphs into a dogma: an exclusivist ideology (scientism). In many people's minds, it assumes its location within a 'Closed World System'. Taylor captures the potency of its ideology.

> We can come to see the growth of civilization, or modernity, as synonymous with the laying out of a closed immanent frame; within this civilized values develop, and a single-minded focus on the human good, aided by the fuller and fuller use of scientific reason, permits the greatest flourishing possible of human beings.... What emerges from all this is that we can either see the transcendent as a threat, a dangerous temptation, a distraction, or an obstacle to our greatest good. (C. Taylor, 2007, 548)

What are the markers or assumptions of the scientism outlook that weaves its way through culture? Perhaps the following succinct five points can assist our inquiry into the matter. By defining scientism here, it will help develop our strategy to escape nihilism.

a. The Epistemological Claim: No knowledge is deemed valid or justified unless its claims can be tested and verified empirically through experimentation, observation and repetition. This criterion is part of an intellectual infrastructure which controls the way people think, argue, infer, and make sense of things. Truth claims that do not submit to this kind of scrutiny become irrelevant, invalid, or unacceptable. This principle of knowledge is heavily weighted or biased towards the instrumental and mechanistic. It sometimes leads us towards more trivial goals in research, because of its attraction to a greater degree of supposed *certainty,* especially of the mathematical type.

b. The Utopian Sentiment: Science is seen as the futuristic guide to human *progress,* both intellectually and culturally. The past tradition, especially that influenced by Christian religion (or any religion for that matter), is taken as false opinion and superstition (*even dangerous*). It is seen as detrimental to, or restrictive of, human progress. The growth of scientific knowledge is thought to guarantee social and political progress—humans are seen to be flourishing and getting better, living longer because of advances in science, technology and medicine. Scientism inherently assumes a warfare model in the science-religion relationship, a posture that began mid-nineteenth century (C. A. Russell, Cross-currents, 1985). It assumes that as science advances, religion is culturally displaced, demoted in importance to the point of redundancy and irrelevance. The progress myth entailed in scientism reaches a rather utopian pitch at times. This extreme optimism is the tone we often find in *Wired Magazine*, or the *Humanist Manifesto*. Quentin Schultze speaks to this in his *Habits of the High-Tech Heart* (2002). There is a fair amount of denial of the problems that emerge with new technology, or ethical issues that emerge with scientific advances in genetics, robotics or neuroscience. Here's a statement that captures the sentiment of super optimism.

> The next century can and should be the humanist century. Dramatic scientific, technological, and ever-accelerating social and political changes crowd our awareness. We have virtually conquered the planet, explored the moon, overcome the natural limits of travel and communication; we stand at the dawn of a new age.... Using technology wisely, we can control our environment, conquer poverty, markedly reduce disease, extend our lifespan, significantly modify our behavior, and alter the course of human evolution. (Humanist Manifesto II, 5)

c. Intellectual Exclusion or Hegemony: Insights from the humanities, philosophy and theology are treated with the hermeneutics of suspicion. Scientific rationalism dismisses faith as mere fideism (belief without good reasons, or a posture that goes against the evidence) or a form of irrationality (outside the rational grasp of mankind). To be poetic is taken to be trivial or irrelevant. Scientism pits truth against both beauty and goodness. Its inherent materialism entails that "science" refuses mystery, the metaphysical or anything transcendent, the miraculous, even the metaphorical or *epiphanic*. Certain human ways of knowing are simply written off, ignored or treated with outright disrespect or contempt. At times, this can be delivered with a hearty supply of academic hubris, and a posturing and domineering tone of voice.

d. Anthropological Implications: Within scientism, people are viewed as sophisticated cogs in the cosmic machinery, or simplified as the most intelligent animals (higher primates). All human characteristics, including the mind or the soul, are believed to be explicable in terms of bodily functions (neuron networks, DNA makeup, biochemistry *or* physiology, or at bottom physics and chemistry). There is a philosophical (ontological) reductionism and determinism at work. That is, the higher is explained in terms of the lower, mind in terms of brain, human social behavior in terms of ant colonies. Humans are appreciated mainly for their instrumental value: their earning capacity, socio-political usefulness and their excellence of giftedness (Further discussion leads to: E.F. Schumacher, *A Guide for the Perplexed,* 1977; Craig Gay, *The Way of the Modern World,* 1998; Thomas Nagel's *Mind and Cosmos,* 2012). The direction of explanation goes downward and it has a way of dehumanizing or depersonalizing us.

e. Implications for Ethics: Science is seen to normatively provide a more reliable and superior decision making guide. It becomes the new alternative to religion and morals in discerning the good and the shaping of the moral self (Sam Harris, *The Moral Landscape: how science can determine human values,* 2010). In a moral sense, science moves into dominance as a culture sphere, absorbs and redefines morality in *scientific* categories, according to a scientific agenda. Someone captured by scientism might say that the scientific principle and scientific rationality is applicable to all things, all arenas. It is taken to be much less divisive than religion. Religious or personal moral values are to be kept to the private sphere of one's life, but not to be part of public discourse (Lesslie Newbigin, 1986). This is the infamous fact-value dichotomy. It is also important to note here that scientism's ethical outlook objectifies the world, giving one a sense of dominance or control over it.

Knowledge, technology or expertise offers privilege to those in political, military or corporate power, meaning that ethically questionable self-justifications can occur. Such people could defy wisdom and even the law, in order to justify some questionable maneuver in the name of science or simply because they have the technology to do the task (for example, drone strikes, obsessive spying on citizens, excessive accumulations of wealth to the detriment of societal equity, stability and economic health—Joseph Stiglitz, 2015). Corporations are gaining increasing power and influence on the world stage, including their shaping power over the university. They are increasingly difficult to hold accountable and to sue when they harm citizens. Sometimes process and procedure wins over principle. Those who control the process do not always concern themselves with principle, especially when principle does not lean in the direction of their financial interest.

To sum up, scientism is the notion that natural science constitutes the most authoritative (if not the only legitimate) epistemology or form of human knowing, or at least that it is superior to all other interpretations of life. It assumes a materialistic, immanent, Closed World System (CWS), a system which entertains a *spin* that rejects the validity of any transcendent elements to reality. It closes the door on transcendent possibilities or benefits. David Bentley Hart captures the sentiment in his cryptic way.

> An admirably severe discipline of interpretive and theoretical restraint [modern empirical science] has been transformed into its perfect and irrepressibly wanton opposite: what began as a principled refusal of metaphysical speculation, for the sake of specific empirical inquiries, has now been mistaken for a comprehensive knowledge of the metaphysical shape of reality; the art of humble questioning has been mistaken for the sure possession of ultimate conclusions. This makes a mockery of real science. (D.B. Hart, 2013, 71)

Furthermore, with respect to the immanent frame, the buffered identity of the disciplined individual moves in a constructed social space, where instrumental rationality is a key value, and time is pervasively secular. All of this makes up what Taylor calls "the immanent frame". One more background idea remains to be identified: This frame constitutes a "natural" order, to be contrasted with a "supernatural" one, an inescapable "immanent" world over against a possible "transcendent" one. (C. Taylor. 2007, 542)

Professor Taylor points out two different ways of seeing the world within this immanent frame, closed (CWS), and open. One does have the choice in late modernity to open oneself to the beyond or the transcendent, the *more*. As Wittgenstein might say, each way of seeing is a picture that holds us captive, meaning that we do not have full control over it. Perhaps this may seem to us both natural and logically unavoidable, but clearly one view is more restrictive. It can block out (make us blind to) certain aspects of reality by the very nature of how it shapes our way of analyzing the world we encounter. It can shut out certain colors of light or insight. Genuine scientific ways of seeing and knowing restrict our ability to see and know certain dimensions of reality, for a specific analytical purpose. That is appropriate for scientific work. It also involves assumptions, an unquestioned background, something whose shape is not perceived, that cannot be proven or demonstrated scientifically. These conditions generally are largely unnoticed.

For a bad example, a major assumption in modernity is that science must bring secularity in its train. It is a powerful *mythology*. For Taylor, this claim (presumption) is a non-obvious, unproven and biased. It is only one of the stories available to globalized late moderns. Many of us naïvely take it on board as a cultural default position, but it will be critically examined in the dialogue that follows. From within this mental and emotional picture, it seems obvious to many that the order of the argument proceeds from science to atheism (C. Taylor, 2007, 565), that modernization brings secularization automatically. In the nineteenth century, Durkheim and others assumed that science would develop to the point where people no longer need to believe in God or religion of any sort. They would graduate from such *superstition*. We notice with Taylor that there is a hidden leap of faith in this stance. It carries with it a false aura that it is obvious, or a logical conclusion. It involves, however, a moral attraction to a materialistic *spin* on reality, a moral outlook: where God and religion is at the bottom of important things to consider.

Scientism of this sort is not based on scientific facts, despite the fact that it takes some of its inspiration from the epistemological success of empirical science. Thus, we see that it is in fact presumptuous rather than cogent or logically consistent. The heavy focus is on human goods, on human flourishing in the time-space-energy-matter, merely physical realm: rights, economic welfare, health, equality, and democracy. Taylor clarifies the point:

> We can come to see the growth of civilization, or modernity, as synonymous with laying out of a closed immanent frame; within this civilized values develop, and a single-minded focus on the human good aided by a fuller and fuller use of scientific reason, permits the greatest flourishing possible of human beings. Religion not only menaces these goals with its fanaticism, but it also undercuts reason, which comes to be seen as rigorously requiring scientific materialism. (C. Taylor, 2007, 548)

As already stated, we currently live with competing views in operation. Our culture pulls us in both directions: both secular and religious. This is evidenced by literary greats like Blake, Goethe, Dostoyevski, Gerard Manley Hopkins, or Milosz. People navigate through early and late modernity with different outcomes in their journey. Many top scientists also have a strong faith in God—some researchers claim a figure as high as forty percent in North America. The struggle for belief is dynamic, in process, never definitively won or lost. This is the major theme of the insightful dialogue in the CBC Ideas program produced by David Cayley called *After Atheism*.

Taylor notices that we know of both outcomes, as we see today in university students and faculty, as well as in society at large. Sometimes they traverse from atheist to theist. At other times, they move from theist to atheist in their spiritual journey at various stages of life. It is not as predictable, or inevitable, as some might want to believe. We will provide stories that illustrate this in Part 2.

> a. Some opt for the ordered, impersonal universe, whether in the scientistic-materialistic form, or in a more spiritualized variant, feel the imminent loss of a world of beauty, meaning, warmth, as well as of the perspective of self-transformation beyond the everyday (along with regrets about loss of its positive impact on

> society and nostalgia for a distant yesterday). Albert Camus represents this group of individuals.
>
> b. Others exist whose strongest leanings move them towards at least some search for spiritual meaning, and often towards God and organized religion. (C. Taylor, 2007, 592-3)

So we can see how the scientism outlook can lead us into nihilism, cynicism and despair. This *train* does not go to Paris, but rather is destined for POW camp *Stalag 17*. There is a logical progression from the anthropology of scientism to human despair, a good reason to resist its influence in our lives. Later in the book, we will clarify more about scientific knowledge and its relationship to religion. But now, we get further clarification of the late modern landscape and the play of nihilism from understanding two very different major perspectives on reality, two ways of seeing. These are absolutely vital elements in good dialogue and even self-identification.

3

Two Distinct Approaches to Seeing the World

In this light, it is helpful to understand the impact of two distinct ways of engaging the world intellectually and philosophically: a. epistemological and b. hermeneutical. These two perspectives emerged as a helpful talking point in a recent lecture and discussion on Middle European History at St. John's College, University of British Columbia. A professor of Polish descent from Rice University had a vastly different perspective (hermeneutical) to those who favored the British (epistemological) way of seeing this post-World War II history. They had a different take on the same events. It was fascinating to observe that they had two radically different interpretations of the same period of development in Middle Europe since the Cold War. One was much more judgmental. Can you guess which one? Each included and excluded key data and judged events differently. This distinction is relevant to our study of nihilism. We now look at the two different perspectives that co-exist within late modernity. The people who operate within them often radically misunderstand each other. It can be quite divisive in our universities.

a. The Epistemological Approach

The set of priority relations within this picture often tends towards a closed world position (CWS). Its assumptions include the following with proponents like Descartes, Locke, and Hume:

i. Knowledge of self and its status comes before knowledge of the world (things) and others.

ii. Knowledge of reality is a neutral fact before we attribute value to it.

iii. Knowledge of things of the natural order comes before any theoretical invocations or any transcendence (which is thereby problematized, doubted or repressed). This approach tends to write issues and dimensions of transcendence out of the equation from the beginning.

Within this view, the individual is paramount and certainty is within the mind (Descartes). The self is an independent, disengaged subject, reflexively controlling its own thought processes, self-responsibly. Sometimes it is referred to as the God's-eye viewpoint. Philosopher Calvin Schrag *(The Self After Postmodernity,* 1997, 25*)* notes this about Modernist cognition:

> That it proceeds from a transparent *cogito* struggling to apprehend itself and the variegated furniture of the universe as unblemished *cogitata,* oriented toward a theoretical grounding of all knowledge in a foundationalist epistemology. Mind is a transparent mental mirror. There exists a theoretico-epistemological paradigm that legislates criteria in advance. Mind and knowledge exist in the construction of an abstracted, insular knowing subject, severed from the context and contingencies out of which knowledge of self and world arise. Self as an abstracted epistemological pivot, a temporal zero-point origin of cognition, is wrested from the lived-experiences of a speaking and narrating self that always already understands itself in its speech and narration.

The oft-presumed neutrality of this view is an open question. The way of seeing is in fact a heavily value-laden approach. It offers a whole construction of identity, society and reality with its own distinctive priorities, values and biases. This is how Taylor defines the *buffered self* (the self over against the world).

Philosophical materialism, in point of fact, is an *aesthetic* construction, not a view arising from science. It is a story many of us tell ourselves as late moderns about the entire cosmos and our place within it, our value, identity, and purpose, often without conscious awareness of what we are doing. Humans have always had a bent towards placing themselves in the context of the cosmos and time. It is not actually possible to do without such perspectival reflections. That raises suspicions about the claims of scientism. But this way of seeing reality depends on a certain naturalistic metaphysics or worldview, which was not always as dominant in the West as it is today. But the question remains, is it rigorously plausible when placed under scrutiny? Many top scholars today think that it is not.

Taylor's contention is that the power of materialism today comes, not from scientific "facts", but has rather to be explained in terms of the power of a certain package uniting materialism with a moral outlook, the package we call "atheistic humanism" or exclusive humanism. (C. Taylor, 2007, p. 569) It works off an ontologically reductionist thesis of materialism, which states that everything which is, is based on "matter", without explaining why this should be taken as true or credible. Taylor wants to question this solemn confidence. He asks whether we are to logically conclude that everything is nothing but matter, and furthermore, that we should try to define our entire human and natural situation in terms of matter alone. Why indeed should we?

Enlightenment of this sort is a kind of *excarnation* or out-of-body thinking, an attempt to offer an extremely objective viewpoint. The self is radically abstracted from its socio-cultural embodiment, and its historical narrative. It retreats to the mind. Purdue philosopher Calvin Shrag notes that we have inherited some of the consequences and challenges of this view in early modernity. There is a trickle-down effect on such a view, which leads to important philosophical problems and contradictions.

> If the only legitimate starting point and stable foundation for knowledge is the existence of an ego-cogito as self-contained and insular mental substance, then all avenues toward knowledge of other egos become problematized and the specters of skepticism and solipsism appear on the horizon. Thus the problem of other minds which reached a stalemate in Hume. (C. Schrag, 1997, 82, 83)

This approach to seeing employs a *designative* use of language (Hobbes to Locke to Condillac), one which confines it to immanence, where language and its relationship to truth are reduced to pointing. Language here primarily designates objects in the world. We cover this issue of language in more depth in Part 2, Chapter 7. It is committed to the primacy of an empirical epistemology (evidence and justified belief), that is skeptical of universals or essences.

What about ethics under the epistemological approach to seeing? Once upon a time, human beings took their norms, their goods, their standards of ultimate value from an authority outside themselves. They took it from God, or the gods, or the nature of Being or the cosmos. But then they came to perceive that these higher authorities were just their own *fictions*. They realized they had to establish their norms and values for themselves, on their own authority. This is a radicalization of the *coming to adulthood* story as it figures in the science-driven argument for materialism. The dramatic claim to establish our own standards comes down to the thought that we no longer receive those norms from an authority outside us, but rather strictly from our own scientific investigations (C. Taylor, 2007, 580). We become the source of the self and appoint ourselves to be capable of, and responsible for, moral self-authorization. This leads to ethical relativism and subjectivism, which we discuss ahead in subsection 4 of Part 1.

Part of this Western Master Narrative is that for proponents of the death of God, they *want* to see God-absence as a property of the universe which science lays bare. Taylor grasps clearly what is at stake in this kind of move and bias. It is, in effect, the ancient Greek Myth of Prometheus revisited.

> It is only within some understanding of agency, in which disengaged scientific inquiry is woven into a story of courageous adulthood, to be attained through a renunciation of the more 'childish' comforts in meaning and beatitude, that the death of God story appears obvious. (C. Taylor, 2007, 565)

Taylor interrogates this narrative, this specific secularization thesis called *secularity* 2.

The claim is that religious belief is a childish temptation and offers a beautiful world (think fairy tales like Peter Pan). Hence, the individual lacks the courage to face reality and grow up into a more complex, cold and harsh world. According to this narrative, maturing into adulthood implies leaving one's faith in God behind. Many religious believers will recall those shrill and terrifying freshman dorm discussions where this position was promoted so strongly, reaching a propaganda pitch at times. But loss of faith in adulthood is not an obvious fact of observable reality. Rather, it is based on a construction of human identity and our place in the world (C. Taylor, 2007, 565). Just because it is out there, it need not be correct, nor need it claim rights to hegemonic control. Why should such ideological scientism be our prison guard, warning us about being shot down intellectually if we go near the wire? It could very well be a mistake or a failure to grapple with reality in all its fullness. Taylor questions whether it contains hermeneutical adequacy and plausible weight (2007, 567). He is not at all convinced that the arguments from natural science to atheism are strong. They seem to include bad reason, inconclusive argumentation, and sometime outright bias. Indeed, they are also based on faulty, unreflective assumptions. We will hold them up to the light.

b. The Hermeneutic Approach

The working assumptions of this approach are as follows and the proponents are people like Heidegger, Merleau-Ponty, Gadamer, and more recently, Zimmermann:

i. Self is not the first priority: the world, society and the game of life come first. We only have knowledge as agents coping with the world, and it makes no sense to doubt that world.

ii. There is no priority of a neutral grasp of things over and above their value. It comes to us as a whole experience of facts and valuations all at once.

iii. Our primordial identity is as a new player inducted into an old game. We learn the game and begin to interpret experience for ourselves. We sort through our conversations looking for a picture of reality.

iv. Transcendence or the divine horizon is a possible larger context of this game. Radical skepticism is not as strong as in the epistemological approach. There is a smaller likelihood of a closed world system (CWS) view in the hermeneutical approach. In a sense, it is actually humble, nuanced, embodied and situated.

Within this way of seeing, one is not boxed in or restricted regarding the parameters of thinking, but more aware of the whole or larger horizon of meaning. Within science and in the humanities, facts indeed are important to the enterprise. But there is a hermeneutical and theoretical dimension as well which is vital to robust studies. How do we see the parts in terms of the whole? Language and our situated context remain salient to the task. Culture scholar Jens Zimmermann (2015) opens the mind to this complexity, richness and breadth of understanding in *Hermeneutics: a very short introduction.* He reveals the common cause in both approaches to knowledge (science and humanities) and their complementary insights. It may surprise some that hermeneutics is involved in both fields of study and discernment.

> To understand is to interpret: this universal claim of hermeneutics is not relativism but the admission that we are not gods.... Both in science and in theology, facts are important, but what ultimately matters is the theory or world picture by which we integrate the individual parts of what we know into a meaningful whole. Even experimental verification by itself is no guarantee for arriving at the correct interpretation of reality.... Striving for coherence through the integration of particulars into a meaningful whole, science proceeds hermeneutically.... Science depends as much on tradition, personal involvement, commitment, and intuitive insight as does any other mode of knowing. The creative and visionary side of science also aligns scientific activity with the creative arts, poetry, and literature. (J. Zimmermann, 2015, 18, 128-29).

Within this open immanent frame, certain hard features of the epistemological approach to reality can be deconstructed and the weaknesses of such features can be seen more clearly. Enlightenment could and does mean an engaging belief in God for millions, in fact billions, around the world. For example, it seems that ideologically China, officially an atheist state, is set to become the largest national population of Christian believers in the world.

The epistemological way of seeing is definitely a more myopic possibility with some fatal flaws. Thomas Nagel (2012) in *Mind and Cosmos* is one of many philosophers who question materialistic naturalism's explanatory capacity. People who advocate the epistemological approach are not good at seeing their own limitations. Nagel focuses attention on our human task of making sense of consciousness, purpose, teleology and moral value—a large section of human experience. Nagel is supported by other philosophers such as David Bentley Hart (2013) and the prestigious senior scholar Alvin Plantinga (2012). They are all quite skeptical of the Closed World System spin of philosophical naturalism. They see through the game that hardened rationalism plays; it has a way of closing down the investigation, stifling the imagination and short-circuiting human creativity.

In the investigation into cynicism and nihilism that follows, we propose to show that one gets more purchase and benefit from the hermeneutical approach, especially as we move beyond the necessarily restrictive purview of science itself. As Nobel Laureate medical scientist Peter Medawar once said humbly, science as a self-limiting methodology was never meant to be turned into an ontology or metaphysics (reductive materialism). It was never meant to be the final word on noble questions worth investigating. When science morphs into the ideology of scientism, it leads to nihilism, confusion, despair and the loss of meaning. It is bad for scholarship and bad for everyday life. Science was never meant to constitute a worldview, a form a dogma or a religion. It does not contain the infrastructural capacity. Philosopher David Bentley Hart (2013) offers an amazing articulation of this serious internal contradiction at work. He serves up a warning for those journeying through late modern culture, with a view to helping them to avoid crashing on the rocks of nihilism and cynicism. It is also a challenge to intellectual arrogance.

> Naturalism is a picture of the whole of reality that cannot, according to its own intrinsic premises, address the being of the whole; it is a metaphysics of the rejection of metaphysics, a transcendental certainty of the impossibility of transcendent truth, and so requires an act of pure credence logically immune to any verification.... Thus naturalism must forever remain a pure assertion, a pure conviction, a confession of blind assurance in an inaccessible beyond; and that beyond, more paradoxically still, is the beyond of no beyond. (D.B. Hart, 2013, 77).

4

Moral Subjectivism, Ethical Relativism and the Failure of Practical Reason

Another key dimension of our current dilemma is the subjectivization of morality. This also leads to relativism and nihilism: with no shared code or normativity for the common good, no social glue or basis for resolving conflicts and disagreements. Taking the long historical view, Notre Dame Early Modern History Professor Brad Gregory writes,

> A transformation from a substantive morality of the good to a formal morality of rights constitutes the central change in Western ethics over the past half millennium, in terms of theories, practices, laws, and institutions.... This rights morality relied on substantive, share beliefs about human goods but unwittingly fashioned an institutional framework for their subversion. (B. Gregory, 2012, 184-5)

In his excellent scholarship, Gregory covers the same expanse of philosophical history as Taylor. The discourse on rights began within a context of a commitment to the common good. It was allied to the virtues within an overall transcendent horizon. Eventually, however, it deteriorated to private interest, choice and entitlement. Initially, he claimed that, "properly to exercise one's rights was to exercise one's freedom and to pursue one's individual good with an eye toward the common good" (B. Gregory, 2012, 197). Today one's individual good so often seems to be in tension with the common good. Rights discourse is accompanied by an expansive list of wishes and preferences. This creates the environment for activism in our superior courts and a strong sense of entitlement by many individuals. Individual rights and the common good are like tectonic plates rubbing up against each other. The myth behind this is a story of human progress and unfolding potentialities, including pluralism, tolerance, autonomy, freedom and democracy. We begin to see how in Western thought unity and identity wage war on plurality and difference, leading to the next point of discussing the character of our nihilistic late modern prison.

Modern Western moral philosophy has failed to discover or create a convincing secular foundation for ethics, and thus for shared moral community. Many contemporary moral philosophers have given up on the possibility of such foundations in our pluralistic Western societies. They see it as futile even if they do not necessarily believe in a hard relativism. Noted moral philosopher Alasdair MacIntyre writes:

> Modern moral philosophy has miscarried its central objective. Not only has it failed to stem the subjectivization of morality;... it has augmented it in a secular, rationalist register. This failure has quite properly marginalized professional moral philosophy, at least as currently institutionalized, as a realistic resource for resolving any ethical disagreements, because it has no indication of being able to do anything but perpetuate them. (quoted by B. Gregory, 2012, 220)

Brad Gregory concludes from his deep structure cultural analysis that we are currently left with a major dilemma of increasing fragmentation and tribalism. The language of rights has broken down, deteriorated philosophically within the immanent frame of materialistic naturalism. This is another tragic dimension of our current captivity. It contains a shocking logical consequence of the materialism under discussion: our very language of human rights is in jeopardy of collapse.

> The commitments to metaphysical naturalism and ideological scientism that govern "public reason" dictate a conception of reality that prevents the grounding of any morality at all.... If metaphysical naturalism is true then human rights are not and cannot be real, natural or discovered. They are at most constructed conventions or useful fictions, but intellectually they are unwarranted remnants from a rejected conception of reality. (B. Gregory, 2012, 224-5)

Gregory raises questions about such attitudes, "the blithe and incoherent denial of the category of truth in the domain of human morality, values, and meaning among many academics. It is frequently alleged that all human meaning, morality and values can be nothing more than whatever human beings of different times and cultures subjectively and contingently construct for themselves" (B. Gregory, 2012, 18). This gives us some important issues to wrestle with in the dialogue that follows. One profound and pressing problem confronts us: How are we to ground truth claims about morality and values amidst the swarms of incompatible, shifting assertions about them? Gregory further ponders, "What sort of public life or common culture is possible in societies whose members share even fewer substantive beliefs, norms and values save for a nearly universal embrace of consumerist acquisitiveness" (B. Gegory, 2012, 20). This dilemma he articulates as our fragmented state of *hyperpluralism*.

So if this is part of our current social imaginary (faith structure and framework for reasoning, deciding and acting), how does it lead to nihilism? Philosopher David Bentley Hart (2009, 21) pipes in. He claims that the *ethos* of late modernity, its prime ideology, is nihilism, the belief in nothingness or *absence*. By this, he means that, "there is no substantial criterion by which to judge our choices higher than the unquestioned good of free choice itself, and that therefore all judgment, divine no less than human, is in some sense [taken as] an infringement upon our freedom." Some would decry it as the *blasphemy of autonomy*: the outrageous claim that each individual not only is autonomous, but should be autonomous (self-legislating). This is also known as the *ethics of authenticity*. If I feel good about it, it must be right and good. Others like Nietzsche celebrate it as a release. Choice itself, not what we choose or why we choose, is the primary good which seems to trump all contenders. The chief value of our age is "the inviolable liberty of personal volition, the right to decide for ourselves what we believe, want, need, own, or serve." (D.B. Hart, 2009, 21) This indeed is the lively road to nihilism which includes many travelers.

It is the thought environment in which we live and move and have our being. Many today, especially those of an anarchist bent, are attracted to moral subjectivism as supportive of their autonomy. They want to personally control what is right and wrong, what is morally good for them and their tribe. We will see the anarchistic bent in Foucault's understanding of the aesthetic self in Part 2, Chapter 5. It includes the assumption that moral convictions are a matter of creative, artistic self-construction. In other words, this means that what makes something morally right is that an individual chooses and accepts it as right, or perhaps even champions that view or behavior—*art for art's sake*.

If they are unaccountable for any overarching norms or codes, they feel free to express and rationalize a large variety of personal desires and behavior, even if offensive to society at large. They wish to keep society, the government, and the church from becoming too overweening and imperialistic in their private life. Canada once had a Prime Minister, Pierre Trudeau, who spoke in these tones. Superficially, it feels noble and progressive to tolerate others, even if you think, "I don't particularly like their viewpoint, and consider their behavior really offensive, but what can I say, it's a free country." Self-construction, as we will see later in Foucault's aesthetic self, is a key value for many in late modernity. It is not a neutral choice towards self-fulfillment, but a commitment to justify one's behavior under the aegis of a work of art, a strong sentiment rooted in Nietszche. Yet this perspective on self and definition of freedom as an end in itself can lead into our current prison camp of nihilism. We will show that many are ironically trapped by their own viewpoint of liberation.

The myth of autonomy hides a dark secret that many tend to miss. What is less well understood about moral subjectivism is that it leads to the corruption of morality itself. It is riddled with self-contradictions and undesirable collateral damage. This includes significant logical and practical absurdities. What practical reasons or motivation would there be to get along with one's neighbor? Will we eventually have to call mass shootings in theatres and schools a personal form of *expressivism*? How appropriate are those tweets where we empty our spleen against someone? Relativism and subjectivism can encourage people to justify their darkest, most antisocial motives and carry out heinous acts of violence. Would we be forced to assess opposite expressions such as kindness and violent exploitation as equally valid or noble, dissolving the distinction between vice and virtue? Even terrorism could be justified, given the right spin on my personal jihadi rights as a freedom fighter.

Modernity locates human identity immanently within the world, and prominently at the center of the world. The modern self is an "imperial ego", the endlessly acquisitive conqueror and pioneer. Over the centuries, this has led to the discovery of multiple non-Western cultures and the hegemony of Western expansion. Christopher Columbus is the great symbol of the modern self as one born to conquer and to search the world for wealth and trade. Currently, he is seen to be a villain to by post-colonialist scholars. Consequences of this heroic mastery included wicked violence against native cultures, despoiling of the natural environment, the international slave trade, bureaucracy and mastery over those who were less advantaged technologically–in a word, the evils of *colonization*.

Manipulation and power plays, both individual and institutional, would be all that is left with ethical relativism: the power of the naked individual, tribal, corporate or superpower will. Thus arises the resistance of late modern thought to such power-knowledge. The rich and powerful, or the country with the biggest guns, would always have the upper hand, the final trump card. Might would calculate as *right*. One insight on this point is found in Al Gore's recent brilliant analysis, *The Future: six drivers of global change* (2013, 92-139). He demonstrates and decries the brokenness in both democracy and capitalism in today's world, where the élite and greedy run the game to their own advantage—towards increasing inequity and injustice for the rest. Noam Chomsky's classic quip resonates: "Tough love is the right phrase: love for the rich and privileged, tough for everyone else."

What principles will constrain the powerful and wealthy, especially those who want to remake our world in their image? The few accumulate vast resources to the detriment of the poor, the middle class and weaker members of the human community. This situation has set up huge tensions in our world (Joseph Stiglitz, *The Great Divide*, 2015). Technology, knowledge and wealth can give certain people super powers as Chrystia Freeland points out (*Plutocrats: the Rise of the New Global Super Rich and the Fall of Everyone Else*, 2012) and create dangerous levels of inequity. Subjectivism and ethical relativism plays well in the hands of the rich, the beautiful and the powerful. Noted University of Virginia sociologist James Davison Hunter captures the nihilistic impact of relativism and subjectivism—it leads to a toxicity in ethics.

> The power of the will first becomes nihilistic at the point at which it becomes absolute; when it submits to no authority higher than itself; that is, when impulse and desire become their own moral gauge and when it is guided by no other ends than its own exercise. The nature of pluralism ... creates conditions in which one is required to choose. The dynamics of dissolution are that it dissolves all reality, all meaningful authority, and all meaningful moral purposes but will. (J.D. Hunter, 2010, 211)

In the end, moral subjectivism is a construct, a form of mythology. It is simply not true that my choice and acceptance of a value makes it right or noble. I cannot transform a vice (greed) magically into a virtue (courage) by my will or my spin doctors. Subjectivism absurdly claims to know how things really are for all people—that morals are relative to individuals. Many intelligent people hold this view, but it is an indefensible and dangerous claim, making justice very difficult. This outlook or *ethos* is rooted in the highly questionable worldview, one that rejects any higher moral goods or universals. Philosopher R. Scott Smith provokes wise reflection:

> Ethical Relativism is a bankrupt view of the nature of morality.... We should not settle for a relativistically based tolerance, since that will not succeed in building a moral society or in helping people be moral. That kind of morality forces us to consider all ideas as being equally valid, yet we know that this is not the case .... Nevertheless, tolerance (as respect of people as having equal moral value) would make sense if a universal, objective moral basis exists for that equality. (R. S. Smith, 2014, 162)

But under subjectivism and ethical relativism, the universal value of persons cannot exist, so justice and fairness becomes difficult to negotiate, leading to frustrating moral insecurity, ambivalence and confusion. We need tough critical assessment of the current problematic metaphysical, epistemological and anthropological assumptions that run through this outlook. It may seem attractive to claim endless freedom and autonomy, but it ends us in a tragic trap—the loss of discernment between good and evil, the breakdown of moral agency, and finally, the loss of meaning itself. The real adversary to wisdom in these matters is *ontological subjectivity*: the conviction that an object or idea has no reality outside a person's mind or personal conviction. In this view, truth and moral integrity depend solely on *my take* on reality. There is nothing sacred about this view.

Because morality is very closely tied to our sense of self, our identity and purpose in life, German sociologist Emil Durkheim coined the term *anomie* to describe the emotional and personal implications of subjectivism and relativism. This malaise in late modern society expresses itself in a feeling of *lostness*, an emotional sickness and uncertainty that comes from living without proper and healthy moral boundaries. In fact, these parameters are essential for personal security, freedom and healthy personal agency. Ironically, *anomie* is accompanied by shame, because we are never good enough (Brené Brown, *Daring Greatly*, 2012) and therefore we must always fight an uphill battle to get people to accept us and value us. The game is endless and futile.

How can I trust someone with my investment money (or my secrets) who could take off in any direction that her desires or feelings are inclined? She could use the power and trust that I offer her against my best interests. It happens every day. If all values are acceptable around the table, we can easily become morally confused, angry and alienated – trapped in personal *angst*. Note the confusing pseudo-intellectual absurdity of saying that Mother Teresa is on the same moral plane as Joseph Stalin. How could we condemn indiscriminate criminal acts such as the black market trade in human organs, sex trafficking, rape or child-abuse? Could we eventually be asked to call people like notorious white collar Ponzi criminal Bernie Madoff a genius?

In a day of shifting moral sands and uncertainty within late neo-liberal capitalism, Matthew Crawford (*The World Beyond Your Head*, 2015, 183-88) has astutely noted that we are now deeply burdened with the sole standard of *performance* for our identity, our self-justification. This has built in a tendency to create incredible stress, often leading to exhaustion, depression and drug dependency in a performance-oriented society. When the *ethos* of nihilism causes a young man or woman to commit suicide, we know we have a problem.

Crawford, in confronting the cultural *ethos* of subjectivism, suggests that our quest for radical individualism and autonomy is unhealthy. We are losing our moral language skill and agency. We were not designed to write our own moral norms or live in our own moral universe (cult of sincerity). We need a web of people that we respect, such as friends, family, church and colleagues to help us discern what is justifiable behavior, what defines us as good or excellent—he calls this triangulation.

> Subjectivism leaves people isolated.... The dogmatic inarticulacy of subjectivism—perhaps we should call it moral autism—leaves people bereft of any public language in which to express their intuitions about the better or the worse, the noble and shameful, the beautiful and ugly, and *assert them as valid*.... What it takes to be an individual is to develop a considered evaluative take on the world, and stand behind it. (M. Crawford, 2015, 184)

We all want fairness, equal opportunity to flourish, justice, safety, non-violence and good faith in our business deals, governance and personal life. We all want friends and spouses who are reliable and of good character. For this outcome, we need to recover some kind of substantial normativity, some higher moral goods to challenge us. We need moral exemplars or heroes together with some higher source of moral motivation. If we do not have this, the corporate world will fill the gaps and shape us according to its desires—with consequential workaholism.

A famous author committed to unpacking the social *ethos* of freedom in his work is award-winning Canadian novelist David Adams Richards (2009). He points to a tricky ruse in the contemporary ideology of absolute individual choice. He does not see it as operating in good faith. Richards probes into the possibility that we have run a con on ourselves in late modernity through too easily accepting moral subjectivism. He has seen the violence firsthand among gangsters in Montreal and notes the way they boast about and justify their latest murder. The greatest thing about a conman, says Richards, is that he first must con himself. A con never works unless you con yourself. Are we trapped by our own Machiavellian con game where expediency is placed above morality, justifying the use of craft and deceit to maintain the upper hand? Anyone who has been a victim of such behavior, finds it exceedingly frustrating and painful.

This now lays out a map: the groundwork and the contours of the perils and confinement of nihilism. Next we turn to our resistance (*agonisme*). In Part 2 of the book, through ten conversational investigations, we seek to plan and orchestrate a great escape from the nihilism that has rendered us morally frozen, disengaged from society, and shackled as its unsuspecting captives. Can we recover from our nihilistic slumber and its opiate effects? The Great Escape begins in earnest as we pour over the plans and the digging commences.

PART 2

Late Modernity and the Recovery from Our Nihilist Slumber

The Quest

The following ten discussions explain why nihilism does not have the final word (*Nihilismus hat nicht das letzte Wort*) in late modernity. These discussions invite the reader to rise up from semi-conscious nihilistic sleep and join the great escape strategy. They begin in protest and end in alternative ways of thinking and living, moving from immanence to transcendence, minimalism to fullness and wholeheartedness. We may have seen the *The Great Escape*, a 1963 epic film based on an escape by British Commonwealth prisoners of war from a German POW camp during World War II, starring Steve McQueen, James Garner, and Richard Attenborough. This is our working metaphor for what follows, an urgent dialogue, or dialectic, for our times. These prisoners showed phenomenal initiative and cooperative genius in order to acquire their freedom, in order to re-engage life beyond the camp and back with their families. They saw their imprisonment as unacceptable, and we should as well. We must begin our tunneling to escape the prison camp of nihilism. The adventure welcomes and challenges us at a deep level. But most of all, it offers a huge hope, an opportunity to attain precious freedom and escape into meaning.

•••1•••

Nihilism is Not the Final Word

Our Wager on Tragic Optimism

University students are strangely attracted to philosophical nihilism for a variety of reasons, some personal, some from an academic trail that gives them traction. They might be in the humanities, education or social sciences, but they could also be in engineering, medicine or the hard sciences. Accomplished Notre Dame sociologist Christian Smith (*Souls in Transition*, 2009) depicts the American 18-23 year old generation as soft ontological antirealists, epistemological skeptics (question everything), perspectivalists (mine is only one of many ways to see this), constructivists (tasked with building self and morality from the ground up), and moral intuitionists (my feelings about a situation or decision is the key factor). This is a strong indcator of nihilism in young adult culture.

Viennese psychologist Victor Frankl (1992,152) once wrote: "The existential vacuum which is the mass neurosis of the present time can be described as a private and personal form of nihilism; for nihilism can be defined as the contention that being has no meaning." Nihilists pride themselves in their realism, dispelling fantasy and cutting through false hope. But we want to examine the deeper consequences of nihilism. It often appeals to the rebel inside us or it just feels so intellectual and cool to be in the company of the *avante garde.* We once met a passionate young student who was reading everything he could find by German philosopher Friedrich Nietzsche, the godfather of contemporary poststructuralist thought. For him, the writings resonated; here was an empowering revelation to this young man of 18, or so he thought. But he didn't recognize at the time the significant social and personal costs to this philosophical stance.

Note the strong tone of subjectivism in the responses to Christian Smith from young adults. Is there perhaps a nihilist, a cynic, hidden deep down in each of us? We all have our cynical moments of pessimism, where our dark brooding side emerges. Tough questions haunt us. There is little doubt that we will at some time encounter a nihilist thinker, writer or artist on our journey. Some see it as a logical extension of philosophical naturalism or scientism, as we saw with Brad Gregory: that we are nothing but *matter in motion.* In terms of our identity, are we *an empty bubble on the sea of nothingness* as French existentialist Jean Paul Sartre iterated? Two twentieth century world wars, with their massive destruction and loss of life or property, produced much disillusionment and cynicism. The mass carnage took over the entire world. Ideology leaves us with piles of corpses and broken dreams time and again. For Sartre, all we have left is individual choice to keep us from the abyss. Existentialism has had a huge influence in the century past, even though it has been surpassed by people like Foucault and his fellow poststructuralists. It was an attempt to save some meaning.

Are we lost in the cosmos, orphaned somehow from our true home, cut off from our passion? Is university education today encouraging us to become cynics—soft ontological antirealists and epistemological skeptics? Is it due to the failure of modernity to deliver on its promises, ruining our aspirations? Have we lost the inspiration and motivation for higher goals? Has our subjectivist morality hit the wall of conflict and confusion, destroying our trust in others, even in institutions? Are we suffering from a radical self-doubt? Our highest secular ideals in various forms of humanism (Marxist and Nationalist) seem to have imploded into oppressive dictatorships of the right and the left in the twentieth century, or in unfettered capitalism and the unbalanced benefits of market globalization today. It is doubly tragic when our politicians become cynical. There is always much that could depress us in the news, but we must confront both the personal and social cost of cynicism. It can be punishing both for the individual nihilist and those to whom she relates. One friend who majored in social justice found that reading about so much evil and corruption in the world had a depressing impact on her psyche. It still haunts her. Sometimes our studies in history or literature can traumatize us with the darkness of the subject matter.

We get a good picture of nihilism and its *angst* in Shakespeare's brilliant play *Hamlet*. Author John Carroll (*The Wreck of Western Culture: Humanism Revisited*, 2010) suggests that Hamlet is a mirror to us secular (exclusive) humanists. The tragedy of the bright young Danish Prince Hamlet is that he never found his calling in life, his true passion. He was constantly tortured with inner and interpersonal conflicts due to the loss of his father and suspiciously quick marriage of his mother, the Queen, to his uncle. His was a dysfunctional family. Suspecting a conspiracy, he was haunted by lies, resentment towards his stepfather, disappointment in his mother and even self-hatred. He was morally confused and conflicted, at times even suicidal, living in a constant state of *angst and helplessness*.

He could have been a reformer for his beloved Denmark. After all, he was heir to the throne. But instead, the kingdom imploded around him, and he collapsed personally. It all ended in nihilism, death and colonization of the country by foreign powers. Murder (poisoning of the king), intrigue, corruption and will to power by the uncle led to the collapse of meaning for Hamlet and the end of loyalty, even of his beloved Ophilia, and his closest friends Rosencrantz and Gildenstern. All was corrupted. *Everything* was rotten in Denmark to this young, deeply lonely prince. He was literally overcome by evil, both within and without. Perhaps at some level, *Hamlet is us*. We late moderns are lost and we are uncertain about who or what to trust with all the buttoned down criminals in Enron scandals and the Wolves of Wall Street. We've been taught to question everything, to deconstruct any claims to truth or the good as a hidden power interest. We are cynics to the core and this is as tragic as it was for young Hamlet, who died before he could grow up. Have we adopted a tragic narrative for our lives too?

There are deep problems with nihilism and with its godchild cynicism that colonizes the mind and heart. Professor Allan Bloom (*The Closing of the American Mind,* 1989) noted how the study of nihilistic authors had deep impact on his students—often leading them to an emotional or psychological breakdown. Cynicism about the good, true and beautiful can be highly corrosive. It can even hinder the very possibility of long-term friendship or marital covenant, and destroy faith in good institutions as well as corrupt ones. It pushes people towards soul-destroying extreme alternatives: either embrace or doubt everything. Sometimes we cynics become discouraged and give up on the hard work of discerning between good and evil, truth and deceit. It means that we only need to care for ourselves, or worse, it becomes a mournful declaration of our victimhood. We bathe in self-pity, retreat into our cave, or move into our parents' basement. We give up the battle of life too early.

Reputable psychologists and sociologists tell us that vulnerability, trust, acceptance and love, are all key qualities of intimacy. One very notable researcher on this topic is Brené Brown of the University of Houston, Graduate College of Social Work (*Daring Greatly*, 2012). But these very qualities are held suspect by those captivated by cynicism. Other people are not calculated to be worthy of the vagaries and vulnerabilities of intimacy. What if they betray us? The cynic's behavioral pattern and attitudinal make-up have a tendency to disconnect, to drive people away, thus fulfilling the internally driven cyclical belief that people don't really care. They just want to use us, and they are not worth the effort.

But of course, nihilism of this sort can be a special technique for controlling the world. The posture of doubt may make us feel more powerful as we call other people to account. There are dangerous predators in the world, but the extreme position of thoroughgoing cynics is to trust no one, suspect and resent everyone. Other people, even colleagues, are the first victims of cynicism. The cynic justifies the attitude that others are there to be manipulated, not respected, trusted or loved. There is a sense in which the cynic is always at war with everyone (the *all against all* philosophy of Thomas Hobbes). Many hold this view currently and can lose their ability for empathy. We recently heard from a graduate student at Cambridge who was exploited by the very person whom she trusted to mentor her and show her the ropes of the laboratory. In this egregiously selfish behavior, the individual simply took credit for her hard work and published it under his name. Cynicism hurts because it contains an anti-human spirit. Some students conclude that cheating is necessary to get into medicine, law or graduate school. "Everyone is doing it", they claim. University administrators wring their hands over the plague of plagiarism. With cynicism as one's space for developing identity, it is difficult to imagine how any new ideals or possibilities can survive, or how anyone could impress. Everyone else, especially those who have faith in ideals, virtues or principles, appear as fools in the eyes of a cynic. A sober question regarding this anti-social stance is: Can we sustain a civil society if we buy into such an outlook on a mass scale?

Secondly, the cynic can be personally cannibalized by his own cynicism. Sometimes a cynic can feel special, transcending the blind, naïve masses. But the addictive nature of cynicism can lead into a form of psychological slavery. Self-hatred is often as strong as scorn for others, eventually turning the cynic into a handicapped, self-despising person. Many students who take nihilism seriously and try to live it consistently tell of experiences where they felt themselves sucked into a spiritual black hole of despair. What was cool and trendy at first, eventually became personally frightening, dark and depressing—a psychological dungeon. Once the black cataracts of nihilism grow over the eyes, there is little hope of seeing the good, beautiful or hopeful, experiencing joy, or even allowing them the possibility of happiness. *Thanatos* (the death instinct) begins to dominate the mind and drive the heart as one imbibes more nihilist film and literature, and hangs out with the disenchanted, anarchist souls. Is this what circulates in the Goth subculture?

Thirdly, cynicism is destructive of one's capacity for relationship with God. In the nihilistic outlook, the divine either seems not to exist, or is at the very least absent, unavailable. He's not answering his calls or responding to our texts. Some nihilists despise God and organized religion. For example, Nietzsche himself wrote about trapping the Holy Spirit in the basement and tossing him out the window. Think of the *Parable of the Madman*: "Whither is God? I will tell you. We have killed him—you and I. All of us are his murderers." Even someone who claims to have a relationship with God can experience decay in that relationship due to the pride and bitterness of cynicism. In this case, God is put on trial by the cynic, who is ironically calling God to account for the personal hurt that he has suffered in an abusive home, with no real expectation of an answer. This is a formula for disastrous divine-human relations, promoting alienation that leads to even more intense, long-term and deeper cynicism.

Thus, love and trust not only deteriorates on the human level. It also fractures the relationship between the cynic and God, an alienation that often creates even bigger problems. The true cynic refuses to believe that God could care. The tragedy is that the cynic rejects God's love out of anger and disillusionment as in Job's comforters. But what if God may be the only one who can penetrate and heal the pain and loneliness at hand? We all need a miracle at times. Cynicism is spiritual poison. It kills God and spiritual hope in our hearts. The cyclical pain of this can sear the conscience. It can also kill our ability to feel empathy for others, rendering us even more sociopathic. This came out in a Globe and Mail newspaper article by Canadian writer and journalist Patricia Pearson called *Psycho-Mania* (F4, Saturday, August 16, 2014). Perhaps we have grown too accustomed to sociopathic, anti-social tendencies in our entrepreneurs, political leaders and reality television stars.

Is there a remedy for such cynicism? We contend that late moderns should set up a *resistance* to nihilism in order to have a better human experience. It cannot have the last word, but must come under critical examination. Together with Victor Frankl and many other top scholars like Oxford philosopher Iris Murdoch, we believe that humans need hope and meaning in order to flourish. They need to believe in the good and their capacity to make a difference, the possibility of reform and of personal transformation and healing. Humans deeply need intimacy, vulnerability and support from other people in order to confront their shame, and find their fullest meaning. Oxford English scholar C.S. Lewis profoundly captures the delicacy of the issue at hand with this stark warning against wallowing in a jaded abyss of nihilism.

> To love at all is to be vulnerable. Love anything, and your heart will certainly be wrung and possibly be broken. If you want to make sure of keeping it intact, you must give your heart to no one, not even to an animal. Wrap it carefully round with hobbies and little luxuries; avoid all entanglements; lock it up safe in the casket or coffin of your selfishness. But in that casket—safe, dark, motionless, airless—it will change. It will not be broken; it will become unbreakable, impenetrable, irredeemable. The alternative to tragedy, or at least to the risk of tragedy, is damnation. The only place outside of Heaven where you can be perfectly safe from all the dangers and perturbations of love is Hell. (C.S. Lewis, *The Four Loves*, 1974, 111-12)

The nihilist not only points out evil and suffering in the world, but goodness, compassion and joy become casualties as well. They can make a hellish, self-righteous, judgmental nest for themselves.

To embrace good and evil together, as Nietzsche did, out of avoidance of guilt and shame, courts existential, moral and political disaster. It creates an ambivalent cultural dungeon of despair, a space for personal depression. David Bentley Hart respects the fact that at least Nietzsche "had the good manners to despise Christianity, in large part, for what it actually was—above all, for its devotion to an ethics of compassion" (D.B. Hart, 2009, 6). He hated Christianity for its concern for the weak, the outcast, and the diseased. Poetic writer and mother of six Ann Voskamp in her pursuit of genuine joy notes: "The cynics, they can only speak of the dark, of the obvious, and this is not hard. For all its supposed sophistication, it's cynicism that's simplistic. In a fallen world, how profound it is to see the cracks." (A. Voskamp, 2011).

Moral subjectivism entails the "nonexistence of the transcendence of any standard of the good that has the power (or the right) to order our desires toward the higher end" (D.B. Hart, 2009, 22). A perfectly consistent ethics of choice would ultimately erase any meaningful distinction between good and evil, compassion and cruelty, love and hatred, reverence and transgression (D.B. Hart, 2009, 23). Many European philosophers are willing to identify themselves as nihilists, however hard it may be to live it consistently. They try to live with a rejection of any source of ultimate truth transcendent of self or world, anything beyond the immanent time-space-energy-matter forces, and similar forces within society. But are they painting themselves into a harmful corner?

French philosophical anthropologist René Girard, teaching for some years at Stanford University, boldly exposes this aspect of Nietzsche's dark heritage. It is that the weak and the victim do not matter and should not be protected and ought to be used as a scapegoat for the ills of society (R. Girard, 2002, 170f). In this sense, nihilism is true to form as an anti-humanism. It denies the possibility of significance and close relationships, basic human trust and dignity that are required for human flourishing. Cynics also turn on each other as powerfully depicted in Sartre's famous play *No Exit*. In this play, the characters are continuously playing manipulative games between the three of them. It is heart wrenching to watch. One person attempts to leave. The door opens, but she cannot bring herself to exit. The psychological trap has secured the three in this endless, mutually manipulative hell. Are we willing to settle for a worldview where it comes down to 'manipulate or be manipulated'?

If we pay attention to what kept alive French late modern philosopher Emmanuel Lévinas in his Gulag camp, it was not resentment, cynicism or hatred for the guards. It was the transcendent meaning of seeing his wife again, living for her and their loving reunion someday, the possibility of a future beyond the current misery. Hope is very important to human psychological health. While others perished from daily abuse, oppression and despair, Lévinas put his hope on a positive vision of the future. This led him to develop the whole ethical theory of personal responsibility, which entails a sense of infinite responsibility for the other (*l'autri*), a concern that inter-human relationships have an ultimate priority. Communal moral meaning kept him alive, ethics lived in the presence of another. Ann Voskamp (2011) answers in antiphonal fashion to her previous statement: "The sages and prophets, the disciples and revolutionaries, they are the ones up on the ramparts, up on the wall pointing to the dawn of the new Kingdom coming, pointing to the light that breaks through all things broken, pointing to redemption always rising and to the Blazing God who never sleeps." Miraslov Volf (2015, 206) adds a complementary note: "The right kind of love for the right kind of God bathes our world in the light of transcendent glory and turns it into a theatre of joy."

Nihilism cannot have the last word. Life is difficult and there is no quick fix, no easy formula that makes everything all better. To be human in our world (a very good, but also broken world, riddled with injustice and unfairness) means that we often witness and experience hardship, pain and suffering, even violence against our neighbor or ourselves. What are we to think of this senseless violence swallowing the innocent, cutting short the whole life potential of a child soldier? It raises a lot of questions for us: Will the killing and displacement and destruction in many places ever cease? Does God really care? Is he really good? Violence erupts again and again around the globe and at home. It knows no borders.

Reality hurts us, and it burdens us deeply at times. The choices we have to make, the risks that we have to take, the relationships to be negotiated, the responsibilities that have to be carried are not a walk in the park. Life is hard as Scott Peck underlines. Teenagers and young adults feel this intensely in the pressure to succeed in education and life, to look good and be popular. The formula we learn early in life often breaks down, and then we have to rethink everything. To be human is to experience disappointments and broken dreams. We don't always get what we want, even when we train for it all the way to a PhD. There are no guarantees of high correlation between aim and achievement, expectation and event, merit and honor. Few avoid heartbreak, suffering and even brokenness. To live is to suffer and to be disappointed. Sometimes tragically, it occurs at the hands of those we love and trust the most. To love wholeheartedly is to be vulnerable and to risk. As C.S. Lewis wrote, there is no love without suffering. This can cause confusion, stress and even mild trauma. But it can also create the space in which true wisdom and character gradually emerge. Some learn to make it work for them and for the good of others as many of our veterans did returning from the gruesome theatre of war. They become more creative, compassionate, and sympathetic. They start schools and construct institutions to help the handicapped or the disadvantaged.

The critical issue seems to be our response to the painful and disappointing experiences of life. How do we negotiate that troubled terrain? Many of us try the less responsible route. We attempt to avoid suffering at all costs. In order to mature, however, we must find meaning in our suffering and grow from it and through it. This is the way of health, taking courageous responsibility to find answers to life's problems, to confront the big questions. We can willingly seek help, collaborate, grow and learn from our mentors and wise counselors, work through our pain, doubts and questions. We are wise to rethink, revise, re-approach, take time to heal and re-engage life, but never to give up.

Some of the great treasures of our human existence emerge when we are willing to dig deeper than we ever thought possible, drill down into our pain to find hope and meaning, to find a place of embrace. This is a genuine spiritual quest if we have the courage to take on the challenge. The narcissists of our day tempt us to give up, accept easy answers, blame someone else, skirt around our problems, or throw in the towel. This approach offers a road to neurosis, un-health, perpetual immaturity and superficiality. Technology won't work either. It won't make us more human or bypass all the pain. The pain is there to teach us wisdom if we have the temerity to stop and listen (Tom McLeish, *Faith and Wisdom in Science*, 2014, 102-48). No deeper character will emerge without learning the art of negotiating suffering, wrestling with its deeper meaning, discovering the deeper person we can become, as we see creativity emerge out of chaos. Otherwise, we will continue to grab onto the nearest superficial self-help technique or guru, burn with anger and resentment, or live a cliché. Suffering initiates us into a new kind of school.

Deconstruction only goes so far, and then we are left with ashes. Without a sound worldview, we fail to reckon with our narrative self and live into our story. We can go *all the way down* and find only an ethereal fantasy. It may be chic to quote Ingmar Bergman, Franz Kafka, Jean Paul Sartre, or Jean Baudrillard in humanities undergrad. But what will they offer when we face the greater challenges of life, or when we are called to give leadership, sometimes in the midst of crisis? Are they going to get us through our first depression, the death of a parent, the suffering of our child or even a painful misunderstanding with our spouse? These prophets of despair can only tell us that this is our personal hell on earth, that we are officially alienated, or that all is *simulacra* (illusion). Being an intellectual doesn't make nihilism any easier. It just offers it a more sophisticated language. But can a nihilist even trust her own thoughts and emotions if there is only herself and nothing else to count on? This is the scorpion's sting of cynicism. One often feels alone in the cosmos.

To live an integrated life, to work from a deeper, *thicker* self, there must be a heroic commitment to transform tragedy into personal victory. People who lose a child to suicide or gratuitous violence know how excruciatingly difficult this can be. It involves concrete, constructive responses working from rich sources of the self. That may involve interdisciplinary research or creative think tanks, psychiatrists, support groups or discussion rooms. The eminent heroes of our world, such as figures like Dr. Martin Luther King Jr., Nelson Mandela, Charles Malik, Mother Teresa of Calcutta, Miraslov Volf, Jean Vanier, Henri Nouwen, Desmond Tutu, Lech Walesa, Gary Haugen, Elie Wiesel, Vaclav Havel, Romeo Dallaire stand out from the mob. They set fresh vision and make something good out of an evil or a painful situation, even a terrible injustice like communist oppression or Rwandan genocide. They rescue victims and hold perpetrators to account. They find a redemptive way forward with a will-to-meaning. They display a will-to-reconciliation in relationships with a view to rebuilding trust. They are true humanists, peacemakers, bridging agents. They stop projecting the problem on everybody else, and take responsibility for themselves and their world. Henri Nouwen (2014) writes an important statement on this task in *Peacework: Prayer, Resistance, Community*.

The willingness to take responsibility seems distinctively lacking in many poststructuralist theories, according to Emmanuel Lévinas. He decries the radical individualism that he finds in his colleagues. Heroic people learn to leverage love and mutuality instead of fear and hate. The late Nelson Mandela stands out as a celebrated international example. Somewhere, these people and many others like them have discovered a vision of *tragic optimism*. This includes the courage to go up against injustice, stand up to cynicism, and provide solutions for a better world, without doing evil in the process. Many non-government organizations have emerged with a vision to bring good out of human brokenness, bring justice in midst of oppression, exploitation and marginalization.

What is the source of such tragic optimism in the trenches of human struggle? That source must give them strength to take action toward the good in the midst of evil and suffering. Within a stance of *radical hope,* with a heart full of tough love, they face into the cold wind of adversity and operate from deep faith and conviction in higher principles. They carry the conviction that we humans can do better. It takes resilient perseverance, an ability to focus on the right and just thing, even when it is not the easy or popular course. They seek wisdom and love, dig deep and fight for constructive alternatives. They promote mutual respect, human rights and dignity for all the stakeholders, compassion towards the poor, as well as the stranger, the refugee. *Faithlessness* is indeed our real enemy today, and it gets articulated as things like egregious, unsympathetic self-interest, opportunism, consumerism and greed. These values represent a failure to take responsibility for our broken world and to care well for others. What a difference it could make if we turned our back on cynicism, and made a substantial wager on tragic optimism?

The first move in this journey to escape nihilism, is to decide that things are not all right as they stand. We are not destined to be its prisoners and we do not belong here. This kicks our plans into gear and we begin to work together to get free. We believe that there is a better world awaiting us.

2

Nihilism is Not the Final Word

An Investment in Love

It is easy to be conflicted and confused under the influence of competing ideologies and an outlook of skepticism. Perhaps at this juncture we have to ask ourselves some tough questions. Which questions will best guide our lives? Which questions will give us most traction? Which questions deserve our undivided attention, our full personal engagement? Many would say that choice of the right questions is even more important than the right answers. It is questions about our identity, our sense of self, our calling in life that probe deep waters (Parker Palmer, *A Hidden Wholeness,* 2004; Walter Truett Anderson, *The Future of the Self,* 1997). Do we have a thoughtful, critically realistic view of the world or are we living in a fantasy of someone's invention? In the light of these questions, it seems inconceivable to give up on the possibility of genuine love. Without hesitation, our proposal in this second chapter of our conversation is that we need to invest in love, in mentoring, in significant relationships with those who can feed our vision and understand our central passion.

Love costs us through self-sacrifice, but it also empowers us in amazing ways. It has a way of recalibrating the chaos and alienation in our lives, providing a foundation for healing. Love is a powerful force that can grapple with tragedy. Psychiatrist Scott Peck's definition, love is "a commitment to the spiritual growth of another person." It enhances our emotional intelligence (EQ), creates connective power in our empathy, as we encourage and empower others. The cynic gives up far too much when giving up on love. We sometimes find ourselves in a crisis because we have failed to learn the nuances of how to receive and extend love. We may not have the courage to express appropriate vulnerability or we may be hiding behind a wall of shame (Brené Brown, *Daring Greatly*, 2012, 224). Dr. Brown notes that, "shame is positively correlated with addiction, depression, aggression, violence, eating disorders, and suicide." Loving, trust-building, accountable relationships offer transformative hope, and deep personal challenge towards maturity. The Happiness Research Project at University of British Columbia Okanagan campus, run by Dr. Mark Holder, shows that contributing to the wellbeing of others is a well-documented, robust source of meaning. Top Austrian happiness research specialist Stefan Klein (*The Science of Happiness*, 2002) reveals good news. We can impact our own joy in life, even reinforce brain patterns that look forward to good things. We can also leave a significant imprint on other people through our investment in love. A good example of love's healing power would be the Big Brother and Big Sister mentoring programs for disadvantaged children.

Love helps us to integrate our personality, while cynicism serves up psychic entropy, spiritual disintegration. Love sets a person free, while cynicism boxes a person in by fear, anger, resentment, guilt and despair—building high, impenetrable walls in self-defense. Love, when fully grasped, is the highest possible human goal, the ultimate ethical jewel, a veritable *supervirtue*. As a very sound, long range investment, it is a huge step above tolerance of difference, or bland acceptance of another person. We'll wager on weighty love over cheap despair any day. Many young couples have publicly declared their love through placing a lock on the *Pont des Arts* in Paris. The phenomenon is symbolic of our endemic human longing for love to be real. We'll put our money on reconciliation and forgiveness as a vital life force, a trajectory of healing and hope.

Cynicism is a massive stewardship issue. It is a waste of time, talent, and money, leading to a shattered life, riddled with multiple missed opportunities for growth and leadership, and many broken relationships. Love is strong relational economics. As Charles Taylor has noted, some enlightened moderns like Voltaire have held *the* cosmic trial. They have sentenced the divine, and declared the death of God, banishing religion from Western civilization. One take on us is that we late moderns are the courageous generation trying to live without God, to live *after God*. Many have taken this stance in the twentieth and now twenty-first century.

But is it actually possible, asks David Bentley Hart (2013), to dismiss the very ground of one's being, one's reason, one's consciousness, one's identity, the very ground of beauty and goodness itself? Contemporary philosopher Thomas Nagel (2012) declares that many atheists, including Nagel himself, still fear that God *might* exist. They are haunted by some kind of *cosmic authority problem*. Of course, many others wish they could believe in God, but cannot seem to do so, such as Albert Camus. If God is dead, love seems almost reducible to a human mutual self-interest contract at best: as long as our love lasts. At its worst, it becomes merely a biological, brute instinct of *species survival.* Or is it just mutual manipulation for personal pleasure or economic gain—using others to get what you want and where you want to go? No wonder so many marriages fail in the first ten years if this is the hidden premise, the backstory to our vows. Who can stand to be used in such an *I-It* relationship? This is a crass formula, heading us into a dark, downward spiral of narcissism.

Biblical *agape* love is not utilitarian, but remains stubbornly grounded in God. It is counter-cultural. "God is love. Whoever lives in love, lives in God and God in her", writes John the Apostle (I John 5: 16). Love is more profound than an experiment in relationships. One of C.S. Lewis' key mentors, George MacDonald (*Creation in Christ*), has an insightful comment about the very ground of created life. This quote represents a distinctive life posture, a profound wager on transcendent goodness, a view that we find in Psalm 107.

> The God himself whom we love could not be righteous were he not something deeper and better still than we generally mean by that word—but alas, how little can language say without seeming to say something wrong! In one word, God is Love. Love is the deepest depth, the essence of his nature, at the root of all his being. It is not merely that he could not be God, if he had made no creatures to whom to be God; but love is the heart and hand of his creation; it is his right to create and his power to create as well. The love that foresees creation is itself the power to create.

Could love actually be more fundamental to our existence than we think? That's the wager, a provocative question worth exploring. This divine music has not stopped playing in a secular culture. We are not trapped within our immanent frame by logical necessity. We need not close the gates of our imagination to transcendence. Taylor notes that atheism is only one *take* on the world, not the final, inescapable position for all intelligent people. We need not buy into the Closed World System *spin* on things. The deep theism of Christianity reveals a God who is familiar with human suffering (Philip Yancey, 2000), a being who has a stake in our wellbeing, a God who has identified with the human community in the incarnation. This is a God who has gone to the gallows, a God who promises to be there, with us, in our time of disappointment and broken dreams. It speaks of a God who has experienced our suffering and rejection, our humiliating bullying. Eugene Peterson builds our point:

> God is love. Love is the core of God's being. Man and woman, made in the image of God, are also, at the core, love. This is who we were created to be, persons who love, persons who receive love. Whenever we love we are most ourselves, living at our very best, mature. (E. Peterson, 2010, 213)

It takes a caring God who will enter our despair and slowly draw out the poison, pull us out of the pit. Famous German sociologist Jürgen Habermas became disillusioned with secularism several years ago, realizing that good reason actually requires the inspiration of religion in order to flourish. Otherwise, reason and language become *thin*, dry and stifling. Political theorist William Connolly at Johns Hopkins University (*Why I am Not a Secularist*, 1999) notes that spirituality speaks to the fecundity of existence, connecting us to the world and the *polis*. It prevents our lives from descending into chaos, fear or disengagement.

The claim that we find ourselves making, within our late modern nihilistic age, is that life integrated around God is a powerful antidote to cynicism. Psychiatrist Scott Peck constantly tries to help his clients to take God and oneself more seriously, to lean into reality, on the road to stable mental and emotional health. He encourages people to stop the game of lies that they often tell themselves, paving the road out of addictions and self-destruction. One might also attend to Psychiatrist Curt Thompson (2010) in *Anatomy of the Soul* for surprising insights on the connections between neuroscience and a transformative relationship with God. He sees the spiritual quest as a means to integrate the self, and move us from anxious insecurity to security and hope: "The importance of spiritual development is now acknowledged by many researchers and respected clinicians as one of the most important lenses through which we should view our lives" (C. Thompson, 2010, 7). What if God's fundamental orientation toward his entire creation was one of deep, compassionate affection and intense interest in our wellbeing, as it is depicted so powerfully in Psalm 139? Dr. Thompson agrees.

> The great myth of modernity as it applies to neuroscience is that we can pull ourselves up by our own bootstraps. We can attain ultimate mindful peacefulness, and by extension, cultural utopia without an Ultimate Other to save us from ourselves. The ongoing terrorism, global warming, mounting third world debt, along with our own proclivity for insatiable consumption, should quickly awaken us from that daydream. (C. Thompson, 2010, 169)

Because isolation and loneliness are an increasingly significant element of our virtual society, it is important to remember that faith involves a deep personal relationship with a very personal God, a triune God of communion. Internationally respected author and speaker and former Oxford geographer James Houston (2006) argues that God is the ultimate source of our very personhood. He reminds us that life is fundamentally relational, and that the personal dimension of life is key, more vital than science, economics or technology. This is the way of contemplation (*vita contemplativa*), as pointed out by political science Professor Ron Dart, one of Dr. Houston's former students. Houston founded Regent College in Vancouver, Canada in 1970 in order to complement the best of academic study at the University of British Columbia and beyond, and develop a theology of the whole person. One of the things we need to recover in a technological age is the art of conversation as Sherry Turkle (2015) writes in *Reclaiming Conversation: the power of talk in a digital age.*

It is only a *personal,* loving God who can be asked for an answer to tragedy, evil and suffering, (Philip Yancey, 2000) or who has enough depth and history with the human narrative to field the deepest questions of calling, meaning and purpose. In an impersonal world, we desperately need the knowledge that a personal God has our back. Contemplative Thomas Merton writes in *Man is Not an Island*:

> The man who is not afraid to admit everything that he sees to be wrong with himself, and yet recognizes that he may be the object of God's love precisely because of his shortcomings, can begin to be sincere. His sincerity is based on confidence, not in his own illusions about himself, but in the endless, unfailing mercy of God.

A cold universe of mere matter, power and forces of physics cannot respond to our heart cries, or answer our tough questions (D.S. Long, 2009). The crisis of the late modern world is due in large part to its *theological amnesia*, a fragmented memory of God. God did not die on the day we stopped believing in a personal deity. It might be repressed in some circles, but genuine love did not die with the arrival of nihilism in Europe or America. Love is a river that runs too deep through our history and is too endemic to the deepest longings. In fact, a personal relationship with God has helped millions realize for the first time that they are lovable. It continues to help people confront the tortured reality of inner demons in support groups like Alcoholics Anonymous, where there are friends to hear their pain. It has also helped people to cope with challenging reality of an imperfect and often unjust world. Jean Vanier, who received the 2015 Templeton Prize for his L'Arche work among mentally disabled adults, is an icon of the investment in love and its power to heal and transform even the most broken (J. Vanier, *Becoming Human*, 1998). His work is an inspiration to all.

The New Atheists are tragically ambivalent about God, love and morality. They want some kind of objective morality rather than relativism. They also want justice and an end to violence, but no universal norms. Caught between a rock and a hard place, they have no justification for this claim and they cannot live it consistently. An insightful quote from philosopher Chad Meister articulates this ambivalence and self-contradiction: "The attempt to offer a view of morality in which good and evil are not illusory on the one hand, and yet not grounded in transcendent reality on the other hand, is perhaps the most confused characteristic of the writing of Dawkins and the New Atheists." ("God, Evil and Morality" In W. L. Craig and C. Meister, 2009, 107).

It seems good to re-examine such a philosophical and cultural *cul de sac*. Like Shakespeare's Macbeth, we are often feel like we are led through the streets humiliated by a black vision of history, "a tale told by an idiot, full of sound and fury, signifying nothing." Have our late modern philosophies defeated us, deflated us, confined us, deconstructed too much, leaving us in a frozen, disengaged state of chronic doubt? The giddy thrill of cultural critique in a senior honor's history class can soon turn into the sting of despair in the realization that *I myself mean nothing.* I also am broken and unnecessary. Imagine discovering that just before final exams or meeting your boss for that annual performance review. The cynicism game turns against us.

The challenge of weighty love sets up an alternative perspective and position. Love is more than something we do. It is who we are. Thomas Merton writes in *Love and Living*:

> The question of love cannot be evaded. Whether or not you claim to be interested in it, from the moment you are alive you are bound to be concerned with love, because love is not just something that happens to you; it is a certain special way of being alive.

The quest of this book postures itself with those who heroically refuse cynicism and nihilism as the last word. It brings robust love to the table of dialogue in late modernity (Paul K. Moser, 2009). Our protest has raised the question of love for re-examination and we come back to it in Chapter 8 as we examine the profound implications of *agape* love. It is an important time in our era of globalization to recover love in the weighty, substantial sense – one connected to truth, beauty and goodness. In the next section, we turn to rethinking our view of humans as a species, re-examining and recalibrating our anthropology. We want to confront extreme views. We must refuse to let our problems, contemptuous comments made by others, or personal wounds define us. In tunneling out of the prison camp of nihilism, we are pursuing a higher definition of human identity, beyond mere choosers, consumers and polluters, towards a higher possibility of human experience, and towards a deeper passion.

••• 3 •••

Nihilism is Not the Final Word

Anthropology's Paradigm Needs Recalibration

The death of meaning, at some level, is connected to the displacement of God, together with the substitution of self as the central focus of existence. We want to examine modernity's *progress myth*. Seen as the apex of evolution, the human is assumed to be getting progressively smarter and better in every way. We are constantly celebrating impressive new breakthroughs. New technology has taken us to the moon. We have eyes in deep space through powerful telescopes. We work at the extreme scope of galaxies, nanoparticles and subatomic physics. We are mapping the brain and we have developed 3D printers that can make organs and print houses. Some technology people are working on the *Internet of Everything* (Jeremy Rifkin, 2014). All in all, we feel pretty good about our accomplishments and our future. Thus, we get writings like the *Humanist Manifesto* that envisions unimaginable potential for humankind. What frontier can we not conquer? What problem can we not solve? But this overly optimistic, perhaps utopian, view of the evolution of humans and their culture is due for some healthy interrogation.

We need some reflection on the darker side of the human soul, examining both positive and negative elements within the 'human condition'. This would include tendencies to destroy life, to refuse to take responsibility for our carbon footprint, to exploit, oppress, pollute, ravage, enslave, dominate, hoard and over-consume. We call out this simple shrill liberation narrative, with its Global North and Late Capitalism bias, one that accentuates mankind's genius. It is the one about unlimited potential, celebrating choice and wealth creation as the prime directive. It is neither sufficient nor accurate, and in fact, it borders on harmful fantasy. A dialectical perspective on the human species, one that includes more of the facts, gives us a more accurate and honest story of how we late moderns measure up. Yale Professor Miralsov Volf offers a different representation of the complexity of our world in his brilliant *Flourishing* (2015).

> More than almost anything else, market-driven globalization processes and the great world religions are shaping our lives, affecting everything from the public policies of political leaders and the economic decisions of industrial bosses and employees to university curriculum, all the way to the inner longings of our hearts. Integral to both globalization and religions are compelling, overlapping, and often competing visions of what it means to be human and live well....Flourishing stands for the life that is lived well, the life that goes well, and the life that feels good – all three together, inextricably intertwined. (M. Volf, 2015, ix)

Should we be optimistic or pessimistic about our prospects as a species? Naïveté is not an option, bringing with it great harm. From a historical perspective, we see that humans as capable both of great good and great evil, unusual levels of benevolence and nasty terrorism and gratuitous violence, courageous honesty and cowardly deception and fraud. The great global twentieth century wars and the 9/11 events in New York City, along with the subprime debacle in 2008, illustrate this phenomenon in sufficient detail. Humans are neither totally good nor totally evil, but a mixed breed of mystic and mutt, stargazer and genocidal demigod, liberator and oppressor, philanthropist and Ponzi scheme greed monger. Brilliance, creativity, charm and compassion fight it out with deceit, selfishness, and cruelty. Germany, for instance, gave birth to the great musical works of Beethoven and Mozart and also the aggressive colonizer Hitler, sophisticated disease-fighting medical technology and horrific death dealing eugenics. We also know that some individuals have a greater tendency to evil (greed, violence, deception, will-to-power), and it shocks us.

Our sophisticated Western invented technologies are used for both creative and destructive ends around the globe, healing and mass destruction, liberation and oppression, protecting human rights and destroying the innocents. The splitting of the atom and the invention of the immensely destructive nuclear bomb is another giant leap forward for mankind? The race for such technology and power was formidable and we are still paying the consequences. We have eaten the fruit from the tree of the knowledge of good and evil and we must deal with the dangerous and traumatic results. The honest nihilist wisely admits that we have found the enemy, and *the enemy is us*. We empathize to some extent with Schopenhauer's poststructuralist tradition of despair about the species, the belief that man is a train wreck.

If we dare to be really honest, we all have this dark side to our personalities and motivations, as Swiss psychotherapist Carl Jung documented. None of us do the best that we are able, or live up to personal ideals, values or standards. We all cheat at some level, and are very skilled at the ruse. We all experience moments of raw self-interest partnered with clever self-justification about the nobility of our decisions. But it is undeniable that ethics and justice have a certain demand on us. Honestly, we find it hard to be morally good, as John Hare (1996) of Yale University notes in *The Moral Gap*. Life creates a moral chasm for us, where our morality and our happiness seem to be either incompatible or in outright conflict. As we will exposit in more detail in Chapter 9, we need motivation and courage to sacrifice for others, or to take responsibility for creation and the common good, to own up to the harm we cause the biosphere by our creative endeavors and our massive industriousness. We need help to put principle ahead of power, compassion ahead of greed, to think in terms of a longer horizon.

Furthermore, we all practice the most egregious self-righteousness and judgment as we bully others in order to maintain our status, prestige, wealth or power. We hire spin-doctors to manufacture and massage our public image, or attempt to cover a multitude of sins through our team of fixers. We feel this strong urge to justify our behavior or our lack of concern for the poor, our weak commitment to making peace in the world, as long as conflict is in our own interest. Professor John Hare argues that religion is something we need in order to become a fully engaged, moral agent. Otherwise, we will have no personal peace, because we will remain burdened by painful shame, guilt or embarrassment over our moral failure. We often feel inadequate to do what we know is right and good.

Famous Russian dissident and Cold War writer, Aleksandr Solzhenitsyn, realized something profound about good and evil, about human nature as he lay there on his rotting prison straw in the Gulag cell (*The Gulag Archipelago 1918 to 1956*).

> Gradually it was disclosed to me that the line separating good and evil passes not through states, nor between classes, nor between political parties either - but right through every human heart - and through all human hearts. This line shifts. Inside us, it oscillates with the years. And even within hearts overwhelmed by evil, one small bridgehead of good is retained. And even in the best of all hearts, there remains ... an unuprooted small corner of evil. Since then I have come to understand the truth of all the religions of the world: They struggle with the *evil inside a human being* (inside every human being). It is impossible to expel evil from the world in its entirety, but it is possible to constrict it within each person.

One of the root causes of cynicism is an inflated, unrealistic expectation of others, or a one-sided anthropology. Why do we need such carefully worded contracts, backed by multiple lawyers ready to sue? On one hand, we expect such great things of each other and that is good to a point. On the other hand, we are devastated by disappointment as a significant other fails us, or an exemplary mentor falls from grace. Our world crashes and we give up on civilization itself. Even in our most intimate covenants, the ideal marriage in our minds must give way to the real possibility of contested trust and adjustments to the complexity of another person's needs and anxieties. This is where both parties realize they are broken at some level and carry baggage from their upbringing, previous relations, from personal obsessions and addictions. This baggage causes tensions, but it is better to be vulnerable and cultivate honesty and realism, in order to grow a marriage beyond the early romance. Good and evil are with us, but there is hope.

Need we naïvely debate whether humans are either essentially good or essentially evil? University students debate this on a regular basis. In fact, we are actually both, a virtual chimera. We urgently need this deeper, hard truth about ourselves. We need to tell the truth to ourselves and allow others to see who we really are. This kind of vulnerability moves us forward on the path to mental health. Counselors constantly confront the issue of denial on the road to personal wholeness, maturity and genuineness. Otherwise, people will remain handicapped, hiding behind their masks. They can never reckon with or escape their own darkest and most destructive tendencies. Dishonesty leads to all sorts of addictions and violence, because people continue to hide from themselves, con themselves, project a false image, and live in shame and guilt. Ancient Saint Macarius writes honestly about the phenomenon of this chimera:

> The heart itself is but a small vessel, yet dragons are there, and also lions. There are poisonous beasts and all the treasures of evil. But there too is God, the angels, the life and the kingdom, the light and the apostles, the heavenly cities and the treasuries of grace – all things are there.

Our twenties is a sweet spot for working on these defects of character says specialist counsellor Meg Jay in an insightful TED Talk, *Why 30 is not the new 20.* She finds many are leaving this hard work of confronting important personal baggage until their thirties. In fact, others are finite, needy, and long for healing and they need us to stick with them for the long run. They will fail us at times and also delightfully surprise us. We actually need not remain an *enigma wrapped in a riddle*, a total mystery to ourselves and to others?

This has echoes of the biblical insights from the third chapter of James regarding the mixed blessing and curse of the tongue (human speech). Now we are delving into the area of self-knowledge or *soulish* intelligence. Neither the cynical nor the hyper-optimistic response is a fair assessment. Cynicism will often victimize the other, divert guilt from self, and project personal culpability onto other races, gender, social castes, or institutions. René Girard (2002) calls it *scapegoating*. Terrorism by religious or secular fundamentalists is a projection of evil onto others, a refusal to love the world amidst its brokenness, to be patient for change. It is the belief that I am pure good and they are pure evil—leading to demonization of the other. It is a refusal to take personal responsibility for evil. The victim concern has been also been twisted, says Girard (2002, 177) of Stanford University. Victimhood has often been turned against God, Judaism and Christianity, claiming that religion is the major source of violence, rather than the protector of the victims.

How do we cope with the contradictory dimensions of human beings? It is easy to take one of two extremes: either total denial of evil and our responsibility for it, or despair about humanity. Perhaps there is a third way. We can learn from the poignant honesty of Canadian artist and mass culture pundit Douglas Coupland in his popular reflections, *Life After God*.

> Now here is my secret: I tell it to you with an openness of heart that I doubt I shall ever achieve again ... My secret is that I need God—that I am sick and can no longer make it alone. I need God to help me give, because I no longer seem to be capable of giving; to help me be kind, as I no longer seem capable of kindness; to help me love, as I seem beyond being able to love. (D. Coupland, 1994, 359)

His honesty is terribly refreshing. The realism of accepting the fullest story of our humanity is the first courageous step to getting the help we need to transcend our fragmented and conflicted state of being. Many scholars and medical experts agree that we need transformation, higher goals and better ideas of how to flourish. They claim that multitudes of people in the developed world have lost their way and are living on only half a story, limping along with an inadequate narrative for life, out of touch with their truest selves—the darker side as well as vast hidden potential. Their mindset prevents them from living to their fullest, and most honest. These shipwrecked souls never find a safe harbor, never reach home or a place of belonging. They are not free as spiritual beings but rather in chains.

Investigative journalist Naomi Klein (2014) demonstrates this conflicted phenomenon in the raging climate change debate (*This Changes Everything: Capitalism versus the Climate*). She shows that no matter the scientific evidence, where ninety-seven percent of scientists agree that we humans are responsible for global warming, a huge climate change denial force is at work lobbying governments and bullying individuals. There are top leaders of industry and government who refuse to see the dramatic impending consequences of human carbon-based economics, the Anthropocene effect. It represents an indicator of the degree of our brokenness, short-sightedness and hubris. Thomas Merton writes in *Faith and Violence*:

> The reason for the inner confusion of Western man is that our technological society has no longer any place in it for wisdom that seeks truth for its own sake, that seeks fullness of being, that seeks to rest in an intuition of the very ground of all being.

People need to rediscover a rootedness to life, a ground for meaning, a robust tradition that can make sense of the full human story. This requires a new rootedness in something deeper and more meaningful that any fantasy or ideology, either optimistic or pessimistic. They need to reacquaint themselves with the rich

Christian heritage that helped shape many of the positive Western values and virtues that we now cherish. Among the scholars that take the bigger picture seriously, there are: Jens Zimmermann, Brad Gregory, Charles Taylor, Alasdair MacIntyre, David Bentley Hart, John Milbank, and Oliver O'Donovan. The reductive picture of secular (exclusive) humanism is growing tired and brittle, both philosophically and existentially. This conversation was carried on well on the CBC Ideas Series, hosted by David Cayley, called *Charles Taylor and the Myth of the Secular.* A number of top international scholars weigh in on the issues and open the field to further productive investigation. They lead us in rethinking the critical relationship between religion and the secular, to move beyond caricatures.

David Bentley Hart recovers an alternative picture of history, offering hope for a more honest and yet kinder world.

> Indeed Christianity was complicit in the death of antiquity, and in the birth of modernity, not because it was an accomplice of the latter, but because it, alone in the history of the West, constituted a rejection of, and alternative to, nihilism's despair, violence, and idolatry of power; as such, Christianity shattered the imposing and enchanting facade behind which nihilism once hid, and thereby, inadvertently, called it forth into the open. (D. B. Hart, *In the Aftermath: Provocations and Laments*)

We need sources of the self which provide energy and creativity for positive change and renewal of culture, with checks and balances on the forces of globalization and mass culture.

> Compassion, pity, and charity, as we understand and cherish them, are not objects found in nature, like trees or butterflies or academic philosophers, but are historically contingent conventions of belief and practice, formed by cultural convictions that need not have arisen at all … shaped by Christianity's moral premises: the ideals of justice for the oppressed, … the doctrine of God's universal love, its exaltation of forgiveness over condemnation. (D.B. Hart, 2009, 17).

Some wonderful fulfillment can be had in painting a great work of art or winning the national math prize or the Nobel Prize in economics, writing a bestselling book, or winning the hundred-meter dash at the Olympics. Perhaps this urgent quest for meaning and significance is highlighted by the extremes to which people will go to enter themselves into the *Guinness World Book of Records*. We want to stand out from the crowd of seven billion souls. But ultimately, meaning that lasts must be grounded in a higher power, a personal God, a living and life-giving, infinite source of meaning. We long for the embrace of loved ones, but also for the embrace of God. Even a robust definition of reason, including scientific reason, does not make sense outside of this larger framework, outside of the linkage of knowledge and wisdom (Tom McLeish, 2014).

Ultimately, one must recognize a transcendent horizon to meaning. Hope rooted in God is not false hope, superstition or wishful thinking, but on the contrary, substantive and eminently sustainable. There is an honest admission of the *sensus divinitatis* in the deathbed words of Parisian *grand pensée,* Jean Paul Sartre. He ironically listens to this inner voice about a meaning from beyond our immanent frame, a longing of the heart for *more* to fuel its passion.

> Even if one does not believe in God, there are elements of the idea of God that remain in us.... As for me, I don't see myself as so much dust that has appeared in the world but as a being that was expected, prefigured, called forth. In short, as a being that could, it seems, come only from a creator; and this idea of a creating hand that created me refers me back to God. Naturally this is not a clear, exact idea that I set in motion every time I think of myself. It contradicts many of my other ideas; but it is there, floating vaguely. And when I think of myself I often think rather in this way, for wont of being able to think otherwise. (Simone de Beauvoir, "A Conversation About Death and God", Harper's Magazine, February, 1984)

The annual Easter Celebration reminds us of something absolutely vital at the core of our being, something that makes sense of this strange being underneath our skin. It speaks to a reversal on nihilism, an alternative *word.* Author Andy Crouch says it powerfully:

> Indeed one of the most dramatic cultural effects of the resurrection is the transformation of that heinous cultural artifact known as a cross. An instrument of domination and condemnation becomes a symbol of the kingdom that Jesus proclaimed; an alternative culture where grace and forgiveness are the last word .... The cross, the worst that culture can do, is transformed into a sign of the kingdom of God—the realm of forgiveness, mercy, love and indestructible life. (A. Crouch, 2008, 146)

We are not perfect, and if we try to fake it to become more popular, rich or powerful, it will wreck us. But if we accept that we are loved, precious to God, we no longer have to use masks to pretend to perfection. We are embraced and valued, even in our imperfection, as contemplative Thomas Merton discovered. This is a deeply profound insight. Indeed, many of us long for a means to experience existential forgiveness and release from our shame and guilt. Miralsov Volf (2015, 13) states it well:

> World religions are our most potent source of moral motivation and deliberation. They are also carriers of visions of the good life, which billions have found compelling throughout history and still find compelling today. Central to these visions is the paramount importance of transcendence, of the invisible realm, of God—but not as a mysterious power outside the world. Relation to that transcendent realm fundamentally shapes how we understand and relate to our world and ourselves.

Critical self-reflection has much benefit, pointing us in the direction of hope and substantial healing. More discussion on the benefits of a re-examined anthropology emerges in Chapters 5, 6 and 10. Next we grapple in more detail with the vexing question of evil and suffering. To get out of our prison camp of nihilism, we must tunnel through this daunting problem. It will not be easy, but we see no alternative.

4

Nihilism is Not the Final Word

Failure to Honestly Engage Evil and Suffering

The problem of evil and suffering presents us with one of the toughest dilemmas for people of all worldviews, religions and philosophical persuasions. It is the reason many have abandoned their belief system, and widely recognized as a complex problem that at times seems irresolvable. At a personal level, it often feels unbearable. Can victims really find justice and healing? Is suffering a necessary aspect of our contingent and fragile existence? Is there a path to moral growth within our suffering journey? Can good come out of evil and tragedy? Which faith and reasoning framework will help us make best sense of suffering? Will we become deeper or more cynical as a result of our pain? Nihilists cannot escape the same tough scrutiny, even though they have often tried to transcend the challenges of human suffering. An image of Nietzsche comes to mind, walking atop the Alps to escape the *all too human*, to find transcendence over the struggles of everyday life, the difficulties, irony and paradox of relationships.

As with the previous discussion on anthropology, discernment is a critical factor here, in order to attain perspective and to make progress. There are volumes of information on injustice, oppression and exploitation and this can be overwhelming. A bitter response to personal tragedy or an abusive relationship can easily implode into a decision to trust no one. Our favorite politician lies to us as he is caught in a fraud or a scandal. We in turn become cynical of the whole democratic process and even refuse to vote. Someone sells us on a *guaranteed* investment and we suddenly discover that we are victims of a Ponzi scheme and have lost our life's savings. If a friend, colleague, authority figure or relative has committed such an unseemly act, the hurt individual often opts for retreat and refuses to ever be vulnerable again. The problem of coping is especially poignant for someone who was abused as a child by a family member, teacher, or coach in the most vulnerable stage of life. We wonder at times whether there are any good people left in the world. We don't have to study *avant-garde* French playwright Antonin Artaud to experience the theatre of cruelty. Sometimes we live in it.

Social media 'friends' can turn on us in an instant and maliciously expose our precious secrets to a billion people. The shame can be personally devastating. The victim's emotions disengage and commitment becomes so tentative and cautious. People crawl back into their shell or retreat into their cave. This can be a strong temptation for a person who has suffered a serious war injury such as PTSD (for example, Canadian General Romeo Dallaire). His experience as a peacekeeper during the Rwandan genocide was deeply traumatizing. Stalin's daughter Svetlana discovered that such scars follow you, even after escaping to America. Tragedies like these can break one's narrative, sicken one's soul and dash all hopes of a happy life. We die inside and numb ourselves through alcohol or drugs. We wonder how else can we to cope with the pain, broken trust and the *angst*?

People do respond differently to hurt and tragedy as we learn from great works of art such as Victor Hugo's classic *Les Miserables*. One person will write a poem or a song. Another will start a foundation to help the disenfranchised, the homeless, or rescue and rehabilitate child soldiers. Some write about the end of civilization, others produce great paintings, literature or poetry. The Irish have produced some of the world's greatest poets and also have experience some of the most egregious suffering. As an island, it sometimes referred to as a 'terrible beauty'.

As a default reaction, many will settle for resentment and rage against God, parents, the system or the regime. The trouble with this move is that it tends to demonize others and recoil, out of fear or disillusionment, looking for protection from the horror and destruction. We sympathize with their dilemma, knowing that *victims* can often become *victimizers*. They retreat inside and stew their hatred, and become an abuser in their own turn. A spiritually mad, cynical cycle perpetuates itself. This is the crucible in which rebels, career criminals, oppressive leaders and suicide bombers are often shaped. Many dictators fit the profile of an abused child, hating their parents, hating religion or hating the whole world. We can even become divided against ourselves, with an unresolved, festering hopelessness. Hurting oneself becomes a perceivable option, in order to dull the pain, or sometimes it is used just to feel something, anything.

Such a response is quite understandable, but it is not a solution, nor does it offer an adequate direction for healing. We believe that the trauma is much accentuated and intensified if one has nothing outside of self to hold onto, if one is isolated. If a person has no advocacy or community to process the pain, it is easy to espouse nihilism as a stance on the world. Philosophical nihilism can further harden and deepen one's resentment. Such a stance gives up on grace, promoting a kind of existential death, a death of meaning and higher purpose, even the death of hope itself. Leisure expert Joseph Pieper spoke profoundly at University of Waterloo Pascal Lectures on the topic of hope and its troubling deficit in society. His greatest concern was for people who might give up entirely on hope and settle for despair.

This dark vision is the view of philosopher Arthur Schopenhauer at the headwaters of the Post-Romantic tradition, which sees humans as *hopelessly flawed*. Schopenhauer felt that the only temporary escape from human misery and meaninglessness was music. During the performance, life made sense for the length of the concert. See Chapter 5, the subsection called "Characteristics of the Post-Romantic Outlook", for a fuller definition. Former Archbishop of Canterbury Rowan Williams astutely notices our current dilemma of fear and disengagement in *The Truce of God* (2005, 19). His take is that, "This sickness, while it appears to be a way of protecting ourselves, in fact prevents us from using our spiritual resources to confront and assimilate the pain and guilt we cannot bear."

As an alternative to despair, delightful, articulate Anglican sacramental writer Robert Farrar Capon (1982) speaks about the need for advocacy in *An Offering of Uncles*. He notes that we all need someone trustworthy other than our parents to confide in, to help us grow up, grow through our pain and confusion—an *uncle* or *auntie*. Others may speak of a mentor or spiritual director. The uncle can mirror life to us in a fresh way, and help us process the struggles of life. That person can even help us develop a sense of humor about our own parents, their neurotic tendencies and their impossible expectations. Most people begin to see imperfections in their parents in their mid-teens, but cynicism can suddenly blind an alienated, rebellious adolescent to any good in adults. At its worst, cynicism projects the problems and insecurities of the teenager onto the world. Such angry youths are vulnerable to gangs or radicalization. The great desire is to gain distance from evil behavior, in order to protect one's tender soul. Trusted friends, youth workers or mentors are often the only solace in this painful period of life. Sometimes, it takes getting away to university to gain perspective on one's background. The professor becomes the uncle who sees good potential in the student that parents do not. Opportunity dawns as the adolescent moves into adulthood and learns how to grapple with discovered complexity.

Counseling may be required to address the imbalance of the fractured self, but a healthy person cannot reside long in that space of resentment without serious psychic damage. It is a toxic, cancerous soil for one's fragile emerging identity. An advocate like an uncle may help to get one out of the realm of fantasy, in order to face good and evil straight on, accept both freedom and responsibility and learn to discern the contours of God, the self and the world. This can seem like a formidable task. It can involve many a coffee or long walk on the beach to work through the inner struggles.

We are alerted to this danger by psychiatrist, Dr. Scott Peck famous for his *Road Less Travelled* (2003) and *People of the Lie* (1998). He points out that most human neuroses start with the refusal to face the hard realities of life, to deal with pain and brokenness in healthy ways. Here's the opening line of the first book.

> Life is difficult. This is a great truth, one of the greatest truths. It is a great truth because once we truly see this truth, we transcend it. Once we truly know that life is difficult—once we truly understand and accept it—then life is no longer difficult. Because once it is accepted, the fact that life is difficult no longer matters.

Mental health, he claims, comes from "facing reality at all cost." Most mental illness starts with a refusal or inability to accept and work through one's pain. It results in an escape into some safer fantasy world of our own creation, a refusal to grapple with the complexity of life and to cope with taxing relationships. To be honest, it is a refusal to grow up. We need to own our pain, guilt and shame and work through it, as difficult as that can be. Avoidance and denial leads to counter-productive side effects such as eating disorders, anxiety, self-medication, depression or even suicide. A more recent book on human agency affirms the same thing: Bestselling author Matthew Crawford's *The World Beyond Your Head* (2015) emphasizes that we must commit ourselves to be consistently attentive to reality in order to find true freedom, individuality and agency.

What is a more mature way to deal with suffering and loss? Is there a pathway to joy through sorrow? How can we get unstuck, access healthy mourning, and trust and love once again? Poet Scott Cairns (2009) in *The End of Suffering: Finding Purpose in Pain* offers some assistance in this journey.

> Like most people I, too, have been blindsided by personal grief now and again over the years. And I have an increasingly keen sense that, wherever I am, someone nearby is suffering now. For that reason, I lately have settled in to mull the matter over, gathering my troubled wits to undertake a difficult essay, more like what we used to call an assay, really—an earnest inquiry. I am thinking of it just now as a study in suffering, by which I hope to find some sense in affliction, hoping—just as I have come to hope about experience in general—to make something of it.

We have to find that deeper honesty about ourselves and our brokenness We have to face the pain and pollution that we too have contributed to society and to confess the violence we perpetrate upon fellow humans and creation. This is the process of becoming more circumspect. Suffering reminds us in a powerful way that we are spiritual beings, on a spiritual journey, and that we have every right to feel guilty about some of our behavior. It takes time and courage to be honest and to grapple with suffering. The ancient literature of the biblical Job follows the all too human discourse as Tom McLeish (2014) draws out in exquisite exposition.

The cynic, in the quest to avoid more pain, settles for the emotional cancer of bitterness and the vortex of irresponsibility. Cynicism is a sickness, as we have already articulated, a dangerous defense mechanism to protect us against further and deeper hurt. But we are actually victimized by nihilism too. Worldview intellectual James Sire (2009) astutely warns that, "The strands of epistemological, metaphysical and ethical nihilism weave together to make a rope long enough and strong enough to hang a whole culture." It is properly seen as an abyss, a spiritual *black hole*. It may suck in all our joy, light and energy—producing a profound, draining disempowerment.

We should not be naïve, but evil and suffering need not crush us either, or totally disillusion us. We have to seek out higher, more solid ground. It is not equivalent to our identity and need not define us. We will need a worldview comprehensive and sophisticated enough to handle it fruitfully, because it is a problem that will not go away soon. It will take a proper horizon of meaning to deal with the difficult emotions, and bring healing amidst our personal or family tragedy. We need to be mentored in engaging suffering, because suffering is our human companion. We must be able to look critically at our life as well as the shared life of society, and to retrieve a vision of our own opportunity and responsibility in the road to forgiveness, healing and reconciliation. We must learn how to exercise our freedom in a productive manner, to re-engage our imagination towards meaningful action, to confront injustice and protect the innocent.

Boston College professor Peter Kreeft (1986) talks about this process in the opening chapter of his profound book *Making Sense Out of Suffering*. Some worldviews are unhelpful and even harmful, inviting yet more victimization and perpetuating the problem. They can be fatalistic or say that you earned this misery in your previous existence. Courage and conviction are required to face off with evil and work through our pain. Miroslav Volf's award-winning book *Exclusion and Embrace* (1996) wrestles deeply with the challenging and complex dynamics of will to power nihilism and victimization. His aim was to break the cycle, disempower the abuser, and *de-victimize* the victim. As a native Croation, Professor Volf is deeply familiar with the racism, hatred, revenge and violence in the Balkan states after the post-Soviet breakup of Yugoslavia. He saw firsthand the neighbor against neighbor cruelty. Today, he stands as one of the great Christian dialogue specialists, a substantial peacemaker in our time, one committed to break the cycle of vengeance.

Austrian logotherapy psychologist Victor Frankl revealed some important human insights from his experience at the Auschwitz concentration camp during World War II. It seems that logotherapy has morphed into positive psychology today (Paul Wong, 2012). The survivors were those who were able to find meaning in their suffering and maintain a strong faith view of the future, holding onto hope of a resolution or a future embrace from a loved one. They longed for a spouse back home, were sustained by a bigger purpose or frame to their lives. They recognized the cruelty and absurdity of their situation, but refused to become a terminal victim, to be defined by the theatre of cruelty of the camp. Many others fell under the weight of the evil games of the guards, lowered themselves to the level of animals and died miserably. One freedom Frankl and the other survivors held onto amidst the squalor was their freedom to choose their attitude to the terrible circumstances, the freedom to remain human amidst the horrific circumstances. Some of them refused to succumb to evil and gave their last crust of bread to a friend to maintain a shred of their human dignity and compassion. Frankl himself persevered in his goal to write a book on logotherapy, a form rooted in the human psychic need for meaning. He suggests that we are hard-wired to seek for meaning and purpose beyond survival, what one might refer to as a *calling*. This means that we naturally seek and even long for a meta-biological dimension to our lives, a greater good as discussed by notable intellectuals like Aristotle, Augustine and Acquinas. We will explore more on this topic in Chapter 6, where we discuss the concept of the *hypergood*.

As a group of students from Central Canada, we once visited the museum of the Dachau World War II death camp on a trip through Europe. We took the time to let the tragedy of this terrible Western nightmare sink in. The experience rattled the soul and made us weep over this narrative of will to power nihilism, eugenics, human experiments and genocide, this crushing of the weak and the vulnerable, this deep, deep darkness of National Socialism. We froze before the remnants of the gas chambers and ovens. Prisoners had been thrust into infinite dehumanizing, meaningless and brutal acts, often turning them against one another in a hellish world. Perhaps you are recalling Nobel Prize winner Elie Wiesel's *Night*. Though scientifically well managed and well documented, these camps remain a sign of the death of culture.

The death of God in European society had finally led to the death of man. The contrast with the astoundingly beautiful and culturally rich Munich next door was surreal.

A recent dialogue with a German professor of literature revealed that Europe has long been host to a combination of tragedy and triumph, intense creativity and mass destruction, scientific breakthroughs and bloody wars, some lasting 30 years or more. Empires and kingdoms clashed in ruthless brutality and mayhem. Lives were ground down under the machines of war. Profoundly impacted, the students wept over this tragic side of history as we did our summer tour of majestic castles and cathedrals. Our attention was demanded.

On the other hand, we have a powerful illustration of the hard choices that face us today in the play *Les Miserables,* written by noted French playwright Victor Hugo. This story depicts the power of forgiveness to transform the tragic, miserable prison life of Jean Val Jean into a productive life where he in turn acts as a redemptive agent for others. He allows himself to be reinvented in the most amazing way, carrying with him a sincere empathy for others, especially the poor and exploited, who struggle under the machinations of an unjust society in nineteenth century Paris. He adopts the baby girl of a female victim of the system, and breaks the cycle of cynicism and evil, pursues the good in the midst of evil. Tragedy was transformed into father-daughter tenderness.

Ergo, the rescued prisoner becomes the rescuer. But there was a crucial moment when he had to choose between bitter hatred and resentment about his wrongful imprisonment, over against redemption into a life of compassion and wholeness. The thing that brought him the greatest personal suffering in the end freed him from himself in a way that he never imagined. He became a new and better man. It was no easy decision, but one where he had to tunnel through hatred and resentment. His choice of this stance towards the world is contrasted by the virile vengeance of policeman Javert whose only concern over a decade or so is to hunt down Jean Val Jean, punish and oppress him further for stealing a loaf of bread. In the end, Javert commits suicide because he cannot cope with a world where forgiveness is an option, refusing to face himself honestly. He has become a true cynic, a committed nihilist. His heart died, leaving no space for compassion, mercy or forgiveness in his worldview. He self-destructs because of resentment, even though given several opportunities to change and redeem himself. The picture painted of these two options is staggeringly graphic. Many of us face just such a crossroads: between prideful resentment and humble transformation. Such choices can entail an entire destiny.

Fast forward to the present, where such critical choices continue in our world. What library do we turn to for such wisdom? Recently, a conversation with the father of a political science student was instructive. He was recalling that his son was becoming disillusioned with the fact that so many fellow political science students did not care about the big life questions. They were out of touch with the great humanist tradition and had settled for cynicism. They allowed themselves and their academic work to become trivial, a mere means to a job. Therefore, the young man transferred to philosophy and eventually theology, hoping to find more vision and significance. This is all too common today. Top students feed on the disenchantment of cynical professors, and develop cynical tribes. They are of the disposition to believe that truth-claims cannot ever be trusted, that virtue, however apparent, is never real, and that hopelessness is the only real wisdom. It all comes down to cynical power relations and truth games (Foucault).

Are we nurtured too much on Nietzsche's genealogies as we give up our power of discernment to embrace good and evil on equal terms? Have we lost track of a good or great cause worth fighting for, or an evil worth curbing and mitigating? Have we lost any philosophical foundation from which to discern between truth and fiction, virtue and vice? Have the seven deadly sins—pride, greed, anger, lust, envy, sloth, gluttony—transvalued into twenty-first century *virtues*? This would entail a tragedy of the deepest sort, like Kierkegaard's soul sickness. Nietzsche himself worried that we would be reduced to insects, lose all culture, all higher value. This is a frightening prospect and should stand as a warning. Who stole the usual adolescent dreams of change to a better world, of the capital virtues (Joseph Pieper, 1956): Humility, liberality, meekness, temperance, kindness, diligence, justice, consciousness of the needy, responsible love? How can we lower our expectations of one another to this degree? How can we recover our dignity and our depth of character once again? It requires hard thought and soul work.

Dare we imagine a Nietzchean world? We want to protest this outlook with the full force of the pen. It is time to wake up from our slumber. This prison camp has no future for us. Nihilism will not carry the future; it is deaf to our pain and suffering. It has no discernment for good and evil, or hope for justice. Reason is exploited by will to power, a piece of ideological tyranny, a philosophical failure. Its take on beauty will not save us. It sees suffering as something that needs to be transcended by being excluded or ignored through laughter and denial of its importance or existence. Genuine suffering and genuine sympathy or pity for sufferers has no place at the table of a nihilist. This is the view of Zarathustra, the strong man, the disciplined one, archetype of denial of the human predicament. Here there is no compassion.

Nihilism leaves us more alone in the world, more helpless. It ignores the costly I-Thou involvement with each other. It misses the insight that we need to receive from one another, through the kind of friendship that is key to our healing, key to seek our common flourishing. It shows contempt for negotiation and encourages suspicion and fear of the other. We shall see later that it fails contemplative criteria, fails to go beyond the power of the ego, beyond the sterile closed circle of the self: my plans, my projects and my expectations. We touch up our bodies, dress up our image, choose our genes through a self-improvement ideology, sometimes in total denial of human suffering. It is highly problematic.

Writer Andy Crouch points out something significant about suffering and will to power.

> In a Nietzschean world we are all reduced to waiting for Superman—or, just perhaps, acquiring enough power that we ourselves can thrust back all that resists us, achieving the domination we believe is necessary for the triumph of the good.... The quest to become Superman does not produce strength adequate to master reality—it undermines it. (A. Crouch, 2013, 50 and 52)

In a gut wrenching illustration of the failure of nihilism and will to power, Joseph Goebbels and his wife murdered their own young children with suicide pills in Hitler's Berlin bunker as World War II was coming to a close. They saw no future outside of their false dream of National Socialism, and it had come to its bitter end. In solidarity with Hitler, they committed suicide and had their bodies burned. These ashes symbolized the mass destruction and pain of total war. Ashes and death was the end product of this Nietzchean strongman vision. They took us into a Dark Age of *thanatos*. The Nazis clearly exploited Nietzsche to some extent as his sister protests, but his philosophy was rife for such adaptation. We should be very wary of these strongman visions today, this white rage, nationalism sentiment and militarization. The rhetoric is similar and it is deeply nihilistic and concerning.

What will unite us? Crouch has a vision, a manifesto, of redeemed power, redeemed freedom transformed by love, focused on cooperation and collaboration. He believes that we can empower one another, and discover fresh dynamics in human relationships. We need not be frozen in the attitudes of greed, envy, malice, manipulation and distrust that shrinks so many lives. We are not fixed on the distorted relation of oppressor and victim, excluded and marginalization agent, insider and stranger. We can refuse to close our ears and our hearts to the cries of the poor. We can block and resist this self-destructive *responsibility phobia.*

> All true beings strive to create room of more being and to expand its power in the creation of flourishing environments for variety and life, and to thrust back the chaos that limits true being. In doing so it creates other bodies and invites them into mutual creation and tending to the world, building relationships where there had been none: thus they then cooperate together in creating more power for more creation. And the process goes on." (A. Crouch, 2013, 51)

Rowan Williams (2005) adds an important statement about active, anti-nihilistic engagement in peacemaking discourse.

> The flight from dialogue into self-justifying, self-perpetuating jargon is then an aspect, and a very significant one, of a flight from adulthood, relationship, decision and creativity. To speak to another is to commit yourself, and to that extent to define and limit yourself; but only in that kind of decision is creation, innovation, and thus human enrichment possible. There is a miserable link between militarized politics, consumer society, the corruption and decline of the arts and the cheapening and trivialization of language—in politics, journalism, advertising and worship. Fear of responsibility leads to the fantasy of popular fiction.... When dialogue decays so does language and when language decays possible views of the world disappear. (R. Williams, 2005, 55, 56)

This sort of posture will give us courage and hope to engage both evil and suffering in a fruitful and productive way, as we seek to face into a mature adulthood, into a more constructive future. We refuse to be overwhelmed by evil and suffering. We will need fresh language, new grammar and syntax, new approaches and paradigms for our thinking. Separateness and disengagement will be replaced by vulnerability and togetherness. Part of the answer to evil and suffering will come in the latter half of this book, as we explore an alternative plausibility structure for identity—*agape* love in Chapter 8 and incarnational humanism in Chapter 10.

Next we turn to an extension of the previous anthropological critique from Chapter 3. We now focus on a dialogue between well-known Parisian philosopher Michel Foucault (a constructivist and a nihilist) and preeminent Canadian philosopher Charles Taylor, who we met in the mapping of nihilism in Part 1. Foucault is very popular and influential across academia. Taylor is a scholar who understands both Continental and Anglo-American philosophy. He is perhaps the greatest philosopher of modernity and the self, with abundant wisdom for the journey we have taken. It makes for interesting intellectual fencing between these two great and influential minds (*grand pensées*). In a stark way, they symbolize the cultural crossroads we face today. It will take some courage and curiosity to proceed and to build on the discussion so far. We are getting more determined and more organized in our escape. We are more committed than ever to execute the plan. The dirt is coming out of the tunnel and the infrastructure is beginning to take shape. We are gaining momentum. Perhaps soon there will be some light. Let's stay focused and on task.

5

Nihilism is Not the Final Word

A Critical Look at Foucault's Aesthetic Self

How do we discern the *zeitgeist* (spirit of the age)? One pertinent question we seem to be asking is: Will beauty save us? Mid-twentieth century philosopher Michel Foucault is a very influential Parisian thinker (*grand pensée*) and a loyal disciple of Nietzsche; he follows in the tradition of Schopenhauer. This tradition, which we summarize later in the chapter, represents a major movement in Continental philosophy called the *Post-Romantic Turn*. He is most famous for the second part of his work called *Power-Knowledge*. For the purposes of our journey, his philosophical reflection on the self in late modernity indicates that he wants to renegotiate freedom and agency for the self. In the third part of his *oeuvre,* the ethical period, he attempts to recover moral agency. Aesthetics plays a lead role in defining freedom and morality for Foucault as it issues in self-construction. This entails his response to nihilism, which he saw as the trap of power-knowledge—the destruction of freedom for the individual. Many are attracted to his vision of stylization of self, the moral self as a *work of art*. We want to examine this perspective more critically using a dialogue with our lead investigative philosopher Charles Taylor. The next two chapters (5 and 6) provide the hinge concept of this book's analysis of our escape from nihilism. Located at the center of human subjectivity, it involves a robust debate between the moral horizon of the aesthetic (beauty) and the moral horizon of the good. Which is the more robust strategy for freedom and moral agency?

A critical question in late modernity remains: How does one become a moral being? What are the constituent components and the best strategies? What kind of moral being can we expect to emerge? A key tool for grappling with Foucault's position on the aesthetic self is Charles Taylor's diagnostics of self-constitution contained in *The Malaise of Modernity* (C. Taylor, 1991, 65-67, also published as *The Ethics of Authenticity*). The larger version of Taylor's brilliant, grand analysis of ethics in late modernity is in his 1989 tome *Sources of the Self.* The chart on the next page is strategic in this debate as a grid to reveal Foucault's concept of *aesthetic* moral self-constitution, otherwise known as the *art of self.* His moral vision, for those who are able, is to make one's life a work of art. This is his answer to getting free of cultural baggage that confines and attempts to define the self in old categories, overcoming what Nietzsche called the *all too human*. The chart highlights both the inclusions and exclusions of Foucault's answer to nihilism. It is rooted in his famous *ontology of freedom*. The radical freedom of autonomous choice, the kind of choice that we have been bringing under critical review in this book, is his ground zero. Are we organized by some attracting force (larger horizon) beyond our own selfhood, or do I, the individual self, struggle to organize things around *moi-même*? This is a critical question.

Taylor agrees with Foucault that, in the West, people are self-consciously involved in their own self-construction, and also that their identity, their spirituality and their moral self are intimately entwined. This is a salient insight. Both philosophers are also critical of a cultural over-emphasis on scientific (analytical) definitions of the self, within the overreach of ideological scientism. Foucault offered good insight on regimes of power that can oppress us at various levels—scientism is one. This was articulated in Part 1, subsection 3, under the title *Epistemological Approach to Seeing*. Taylor's thought on the subject is not, however, restricted by a nihilist, Closed World System immanent frame. The following discussion will show how the second way of seeing (the hermeneutical approach) works powerfully as Taylor's critical skill set in analyzing the late modern self and its relationship to nihilism.

The debate begins when one asks *who* and *what* else is involved in the shaping of the self. In Taylor's analysis, there are five significant criteria, divided into categories A and B, indicators of the shape of one's own moral self-constitution. It is a helpful chart that appreciates today's plurality of convictions. He suggests that all five elements tend to be involved in identity development. With scholars like Foucault, it is possible to over-emphasize certain criteria versus others, and important to see the impact.

Taylor's Moral Self-Construction Diagnostics

Category A (*Creativity*)

(i) Creation and construction (as well as discovery) of the self.

(ii) Pursuit of originality in one's self-crafting.

(iii) Opposition to the rules of society and even potentially to what one recognizes as morality, or the moral order (anarchistic element).

Category B *(Social and Moral Connectedness and Accountability)*

(i) Openness to horizons of significance prevents one's self-creation from losing the background that can save it from insignificance and trivialization (destruction of meaning).

(ii) Self-definition needs to be developed in dialogue with significant others, that is, fellow moral interlocutors within a community and a narrative. (Taylor, 1991, 65, 66)

This chart also helps us understand Taylor's moral ontology of the good, to which we give important elaboration in Chapter 6. Admitting the strong impact of the Post-Romantic Turn in philosophy, Taylor understands the currency of the language of self-construction. This is not lost on graduate students in the field of education or gender studies, where self-construction and identity politics are a major theme. Taylor takes Foucault seriously, but disagrees with him on certain key points. He does not reject the Romantic or Post-Romantic traditions out of hand. One's tradition does impact one's identity. Taylor is a complex thinker, a unique cross between a Continental and Anglo-American philosopher, and brings careful critique to both traditions of philosophy. He is quite unique as a philosophical contributor and respected widely as a top world philosopher. Richard Rorty considers him one of the top twelve alive today.

Taylor does not concede the legitimacy of just any form of self-construction, which puts him in tension with Foucault's view. Referring back to the chart above, his concern with Foucault is the extreme emphasis that he places on Category A (Creativity), and the near exclusion of any emphasis on Category B (Accountability, Communality, Connectedness to the Other, and Mutuality). This leads to a radical form of individualism, holding the potential for narcissism among other dark tendencies.

Furthermore, Taylor contests Foucault's radical nominalism, which denies the possibility of self-discovery along with self-creation (Ai.). His problem is with the over-emphasis (one-sidedness) on creativity. Taylor has a higher commitment to certain natural and moral *givens*. In Chapter 6, we will explain what it means that Taylor is a *falsifiable moral realist*. Briefly, this means that he recognizes both an objective and a subjective component (pole) in moral self-constitution, and does not allow ethics to be reduced to either extreme objectivity or extreme subjectivity, especially to radical subjectivism, a view that leads us back to the prison camp of nihilism. It gives up on normativity.

Taylor also questions the merits and overall legitimacy of category (Aiii), that self-constitution should automatically involve denial of the moral rules of society—the anarchic stance. He does not have an inherent bias against social norms, but nor is he an uncritical social conventionalist. Society always needs continued reform. Taylor (1991, 63) justifiably asks why aesthetic self-making should necessarily pass through a repudiation of the moral order. Why are all moral regimes, norms and all humanisms written off by Foucault? This seems a bit extreme. His ungrounded ontology of freedom is held in question as a mere projection. Finally, his concern with Foucault is the inherent denial of the significance of category (Bi) and (Bii), including the idea of moral horizons and the more social or dialogical dimensions of self-formation. This is a very serious oversight that dearly concerns Taylor. It does not square with his view in the whole first section of *Sources of the Self* (C. Taylor, 1989, 3-97). There he deals in depth with the communal and narrative aspects of moral self-constitution. Foucault wants to pry the self loose from relational, societal restrictions and the structures of institutions, in order to attain more freedom and avoid labeling, entrapment or *totalization*. He feels that this aesthetic strategy is the only way to empower the individual, maintain agency and avoid being dominated by other individuals or power-knowledge regimes. There is an element of the *amoral fugitive* in Foucault.

Foucault's idea of moral self-constitution is hyper-individualistic, almost Hobbesian. Taylor, a more communitarian thinker, brings a fresh set of concerns and balance to the table. He suggests that,

> What must be wrong is a simple privileging of one over the other (e.g. A over B) ... That is what trendy doctrines of "deconstruction" involve today ... they stress (Ai) the constructive, creative nature of our expressive languages, while altogether forgetting (Bi). They capture the more extreme forms of (Aiii), the amoralism of creativity ... while forgetting (Bii), its dialogical setting, which binds us to others ... These thinkers buy into the background outlook of authenticity, for instance in their understanding of the creative, self-constitutive powers of language ... while ignoring some of its essential constituents. (C. Taylor, 1991, 66, 67)

Taylor's concern is that Foucault's position is too reductionist, ignoring as he does certain key or important constituents of self-articulation, such as the dynamics of Category B (Accountability). By abolishing all other-than-self horizons of significance, and demoting the importance of dialogue with other moral interlocutors, morality can become quite narrowly focused on self alone: self-control, self-interest, self-expression, self-determination, self-invention, and self-justification. It can become a virtual monologue, an abstract self-projection of one's values onto the world, rather than a source of communal conversation, or cooperation. Social embedding, according to philosophers like Merleau-Ponty, is a crucial concern for contemporary moral dialogue. The mobility of people, fragmentation of families and the loss of roots is part of the current crisis of self that we are experiencing in a globalized world. The book and movie *Fight Club* show the crisis of masculinity for young urban males raised by their single mothers in a consumer society. As alienated youth, they go to extremes in the boxing ring to find meaning and masculinity amidst bland urbanism. They mimic Foucault's nihilism as they seek to invent a new, heroic self in order to confront their *ennui* (existential boredom), weak identity and lack of meaning.

For Foucault and his concept of self-constitution, the clear weight of bias in his idea of subjectivity is towards a radical autonomy (getting free of the world, which includes getting free of one's former self), not construction as part of a communal dialogue or collaboration. In fact, he does not claim that his project is an ethics for society as a whole—it is focused on the individual. This is both a deconstruction and a reinvention of the very concept of self, ethics and morality. It is an *ethics of the individual* (reminiscent of Nietzsche's strongman or *übermensch*) in rebellion against societal controls and norms (*anti-nomian*). This tends to skew Foucault's theory of the moral self towards narcissism. Pierre Hadot, his colleague at Collège de France, calls it a form of *Dandyism*. Foucault does have a very strong emphasis on caring for oneself first and foremost. James Houston, an Oxford geographer become philosopher of personhood and historian of spirituality, writes about the fragile state of the aesthetic self. He is quite concerned that, while it is fun to manipulate and dress up the aesthetic self, it can also become a dangerous handicap. One cannot remain an adolescent for one's whole life without serious consequences.

> It is instinctual to be "aesthetic"—that is to live on the surface of things. We need to die away from the aesthetic stage in which we exhibit ourselves like Hollywood stars—showing off our bodies, our intelligence, our accomplishments and our passion for happiness and living impatiently in quest of instant gratification. No wonder such worldly aesthetes have such fragile and brittle identities, fostered by narcissistic personalities. (J.M. Houston, 2006, 44)

According to Foucault, ethics involves the self in a study of power relations and truth games within the social matrix. Then one must abstract oneself from the problematized social matrix, rethink, and then impose the newly invented self combatively onto society. It is a power move, a pure form of self-assertion and resistance to the status quo. "The understanding of value as something created gives the individual a sense of freedom and power" (C. Taylor, 1991, 67). It interacts with *truth games* and *power relations*. Foucault attempts to deal with the aesthetic self-constitution issue through his strong emphasis on the constructive imagination. His strong emphasis on the art of the self follows Nietzsche, the great aesthetic pioneer. Noted Oxford English scholar Terry Eagleton (1990), in *The Ideology of the Aesthetic*, has a substantial exposition of both Foucault and Nietzsche in this regard. Significantly, we will come to see that human rights are under attack with such a strong emphasis on the aesthetic.

In the next chapter, we will contrast this stance with Taylor's *ontology of the good*. In Foucault, the language of a transcendent good is repressed in self-making, in favor of the language of the creative imagination and radical individual self-articulation—a literal invention and reinvention of self. There can be strong, assertive force in this kind of self-articulation as we often see in national politics of various wester countries. The grammar of the good is rethought and reconfigured in terms of the artistic. Self and its expression are taken as the proximate source of the good and the true. This is a somewhat risky and dangerous form of *expressivism.* A typical example is the young millennial lured by potential fame in Hollywood, who hops on a motorcycle, travels across country and moves to California to reinvent himself in an acting career.

The sources of the Foucauldian self are contained, self-reflexively, within the creative self. One might explore what others (ancient and modern) are doing in their self-creation, but it is up to the individual to invent a new self, something unique and original. Once this is realized, suggests Foucault, superior individual freedom and power, even genius, will emerge. The attempt here is to break my truth free from the regime or the power of the other who seeks to manipulate me. Unlike other conceptions of transcendent moral sources in reason, nature or God, the Post-Romantic Foucault focuses on sources of the self within, in the register of self-empowerment, a continual ongoing re-invention of self and re-assertion of its artistic freedom. Many contemporary films have followed exactly this thematic trajectory, where the character invents a new self in the military or some great adventure.

Such a perception of sources makes it possible to relativize, control and even marginalize others and the social world. The radical individual often cuts herself off from the family narrative. This gives one power over the world, a power that could easily be abused, or even results in disrespect and even violence. One could even become anti-social; at the very least, it decreases vulnerability and accountability to others. Listening, vulnerability and empathy are key components of effectual ethics within human relations. This problem is especially acute given Foucault's emphasis on the kind of accountability that is merely self-reflexive, a responsibility to care for self, first, love self as a priority above all else. It is easy to see how this could lead to contestation. If it is my life that is the work of art, then I, and my reflexive relationship with myself, become central. It lacks a consciousness of an order of compassion and the gift that is the other. The one remaining moral imperative is *my individual artistic creation*.

It unfortunately pushes towards a dangerous atomization and fragmentation of self and society—*hyper-pluralism* or a radical celebration of difference. It postures the self in ongoing conflict with society (*agonisme*), rather than seeking serendipity, mutuality or common cause. It is one thing if one is trying to escape a dysfunctional background such as an alcoholic home. It is quite another when others become a mere object of manipulation for self-interest. In *A Secular Age* (2007, 559), Taylor protests: "There is no priority of the individual's sense of self over society: our most primordial identity is as a new player being inducted in an old game." He believes that we are first social beings prior to becoming individuals.

Characteristics of the Post-Romantic Outlook

Foucault's paradigm of the moral self (C. Taylor, 1989, 434-55) falls within the Post-Romantic tradition. The characteristics of this tradition reveals how the aesthetic plausibility structure radically rethinks the whole moral culture sphere. This is nihilism writ large, and it may not be quite what we want. It does, however, help us understand much of what is emerging in late modern culture. Some of the key players include: Schopenhauer, Baudelaire, Nietzsche, and Foucault. Below are the markers of this European nihilist philosophical viewpoint, the backstory of our dialogue with Foucault and the poetic self.

1. Art is superior to morality, and sees itself in conflict with the social moral order.

2. Humans live in a chaotic or fallen natural and social world, rooted in chaos and the will to power. One can take an affirmative stance towards the world through seeing it as beautiful—seeing the world through an aesthetic lens. This is the only remaining basis for its justification, or attempt towards wholeness, the attempt to rescue some kind of meaning,

however ephemeral or fleeting. Thus, the wager is that beauty does attempt to save us, at the cost of giving us a *thin* self. One takes an ironic attitude towards oneself.

3. Being itself is not good as such, nor is human being *per se* taken as good. It is in need of a *make-over*. It is the job of the individual to accomplish this task. It is up to us (*tuum est*). This can be combined with a sense of psychic and cosmic homelessness as we see in Walker Percy's writing (*Lost in the Cosmos*, 1983; *The Thanatos Syndrome*, 1987).

4. Hope resides in a strong belief in the power of the creative imagination to transfigure or transform the world and the self, or to reveal it afresh as beautiful. This view is much stronger in the community of the arts.

5. Language is a key means of changing the world, or at least the way one sees the world; it is key to one's poetic self-expression (*poesis*) and re-articulation of the self.

6. This tends to result in an aesthetic amorality, a move beyond good and evil, an embrace or affirmation of violence and cruelty (Baudelaire) as well as patience and care for the marginalized (Jean Vanier). There is no logical or moral distinction (hierarchy) between a host of possible values which inevitably contradict each other, producing ambivalence. Nietzsche, however, is self-confessedly against pity and compassion for victims. He believes that creativity emerges out of chaos and cruelty; the individual must overcome the world through self-making. This is the way to transcend the vagaries of society (*the human all too human*). The *übermensch* is the overcomer. With the make-over of the self as the central project, choices are unqualified and self-justified.

Foucault would agree with Taylor's placement of his project in the twentieth century cultural transition called the *Post-Romantic Turn* (Taylor, 1989, 434-455). The *expressivism* of this tradition gives a higher, ironically *normative* significance to the aesthetic culture sphere, and opens a full challenge to the moral, religious and scientific culture spheres (Taylor, 1991, 63). Foucault wishes to transcend the code-morality of Old Christian Europe, with its universal intent towards normalization, via a new morality of the evolving ethics of the autonomous, artistic individual. Symbolically, the French Revolution continues in the battle for the moral self. It is similar in sentiment to the *avant-garde* in modern art, such as the Dada movement of the 1920s, where the world is not *represented* but *created.* Art justifies itself, is an end in tiself. The pressing question is whether Foucault's project of recovering the self is ironically captive to its own *totalizing* impulse, the *aestheticization of the moral*. It seems to be a strong case scenario of promoting an ideology of the aesthetic (T. Eagleton, 2000, 366-417).

There is a strong tendency in Foucault to celebrate the individual's own powers to construct and interpret reality in a context shaped by immanence and the finite (the closed immanent frame). This is combined with a will to deny the legitimacy of any binding moral horizon or moral culture outside or above the self. This puts the emphasis on freedom to choose how one wishes to represent oneself to the world (self-interpretation), through the masks one employs.

> Foucault's spiritual profile [is]: an even higher estimate of the unrestricted powers of the imagination than the Romantics had, and hence a celebration of those powers ... This subjectivism of self-celebration is a standard temptation in a culture which exalts freedom and puts such value on the creative imagination. (C. Taylor, 1989, 489, 490)

According to this *ethos*, all values are welcome to the table of open hospitality, which leads to quite absurd evaluations and consequences. We are back to relativism. In Foucault's moral ontology of aesthetic freedom, a key problem is that there is no hierarchy of various goods. The consequence is that nothing appears to be of ultimate value, and nothing is better or worse. All is flattened with the consequence of a trivialization of higher, nobler values. All becomes banal, leaving us with social and personal ambivalence. The sacred and the vulgar are on one level. This entails the demise of discernment: virtues and vices, good and evil are leveled and reduced to an individual's stylization of self, feeding the *malaise* of late modernity, and a sickness within society.

Oxford feminist philosopher Lois McNay (1994) is a Foucault scholar. She values some of Foucault's insights, but on this point, she sees a very large gap in his ethics. He may understand power relations and sexual stereotypes, but in the end he leaves women vulnerable and without rights protection. The subjectivization of morality has an ironic way of disintegrating protections to individual rights. Again, we feel the sting of the scorpion's tail. Justice for the weak and politically downtrodden is a far reach from ethics as aesthetics. One's individually chosen values remain more arbitrary, with the freedom to either champion them or discard them at will. With this comes also a self-trivialization.

> Beauty is a satisfaction for itself ... gives its own intrinsic fulfillment. Its goal is internal.... Aesthetic wholeness is an independent goal with its own *telos*, its own form of goodness and satisfaction. (C. Taylor, 1991, 64, 65).

Taylor makes an astute connection between Nietzsche's nihilism, his *transvaluation of all values* and Foucault's ethics. This constitutes the seductive attraction of his views to many late moderns. We note the twenty-first century cultural analysis of the narcissistic society by Jean M. Twenge and W. Keith Campbell (2009) in *The Narcissism Epidemic: Living in the Age of Entitlement*. It can easily implode into a raw quest for money, sex, power, debt and unsustainable consumerism. This results in a directionless outlook, not the road to happiness and full human flourishing.

It is here that one begins to recognize that Foucault's project of the recovery of the subjective agency is deeply flawed, threatened by a loss of meaning and self-trivialization. It sets up a potential fall into a fatal and tragic nihilism, with self-implosion into endless spirals of self-reflexivity. There remains no broader horizon of significance, accountability and recognition by others. His project is in grave danger of running out of fuel, imploding into the nihilism of a pointless existence and even despair. One can only take this revolutionary experiment so far before it hits a wall. We hear a warning from psychiatrist Scott Peck.

Does this mean that we never have to grow up? Taylor notes that, in this Post-Romantic philosophical turn, there is a tendency to legitimate action and ethical behavior according to beauty rather than by its inherent good, nobility or social impact. One could even justify destructive, cruel and oppressive actions on these terms, as do power-amassing dictators or people in the theatre of cruelty. Europeans are often more in touch with this darker side of Foucault than Americans.

> What in the universe commands our affirmation, when we have overcome the all-too-human, is not properly called its goodness but comes closer to being its beauty.... Part of the heroism of the Nietzschean superman is that he can rise beyond the moral, beyond the concern with the good, and manage in spite of suffering and disorder and the absence of all justice to respond to something like the beauty of it all. (C. Taylor, 1989, 454)

A prestigious place is given to one's own inner powers of construing, imagining or interpreting the world. The interpretative lens of goodness is exchanged for the lens of the beautiful, or the sensuality of pleasure. It should not surprise us that maximizing pleasure is a key priority in Foucault's ethics of self, including some very dangerous experimentation. The beauty of it all for Post-Romantics makes all things *tolerable,* dangerously so perhaps, thereby undermining healthy relationships and commitments, and corrupting ethics itself.

Self emerges as the creator, *stylizer* and *valorizer* of its own individual values. These are then projected onto the world. This is what gets stylized into oligarchic and plutocratic levels of wealth, power and privilege today. This problem also exists as a significant danger in politics. Things can devolve into a politics of style and sophist rhetoric, with the consequence of a hollowing out of democracy (Al Gore, 2013, 92-139). Note how this plays out in the documentaries like *The Human Experiment;* or *Requiem to the American Dream.*

It involves cynicism and contempt for the public good, a loss of what Rowan Williams calls *contemplation*.

> There is no love without contemplation, no contemplation without a mind and heart open to receive and not seeking to create its own world out of nothingness of the ego and its fantasies. Contemplation for men and women is looking and listening and being molded by what is other. It is recognizing that you are created—limited, living in time—and allowing yourself to go on being created in and by the world of things and persons in time, all of them mediating the obscure universal initiative of an uncreated action, so wholly regardless of 'self' that it lets the whole universe be... We need to live in a world constantly inviting us to contemplation, a world which will not leave us alone, feeding only on ourselves—a world which delights us and which assaults us by its strangeness, its resistance to us. (R. Williams, 2005, 40)

This is a radically different hermeneutic of self from Foucault. Taylor deftly agrees, rigorously challenging Foucault's radical individualism and over-emphasis on creativity and self-reflexivity.

> I can define my identity only against the background of things that matter. But to bracket out history, nature, society, the demands of solidarity, everything but what I find in myself, would be to eliminate all candidates for what matters. Only if I exist in a world in which history, or the demands of nature, or the needs of my fellow human beings, or the duties of citizenship, or the call of God, or something else of this order that *matters* crucially, can I define an identity for myself that is not trivial. (C. Taylor, 1991, 40-41)

Trivialization of self and one's life-world, and trivialization of the other, is quite characteristic of the spiritual journey of aesthetic nihilism. It is a Faustian agreement. We should now be alert to the fact that the language of values and the language of aesthetics are closely entwined. Max Weber and Foucault are philosophical companions. The language of values emerges out of an intellectual outlook of nihilism. Nietzsche was introduced and made palatable to American intelligentsia by Max Weber (Allan Bloom, 1989, *The Closing of the American Mind*).

Value, according to Foucault, is what we hold to be valuable, not what society at large thinks. It is a personal, aesthetic choice. Can we be saved by beauty? We cannot, not as long as beauty is held captive by immanent attempts to achieve transcendence, by an élite self-reflexive few. Rowan Williams counters with an antidote to such destructive nihilism. There is much at stake as we figure out how to negotiate our way through our most vexing problems for individuals and for society. It matters a great deal how we see our calling and task in moral growth, as well as political maturity, or how we function as a civil society: "isolation is the refusal of humanity".

> *What is it to be human*: to be a creature, a part of the world, a moment in a pattern, dependent on others, others dependent on ourselves, called therefore to contemplation, without which there is no growth or fullness. Isolation is the refusal of humanity; and that includes the isolation of my or our needs from those of the human world. Beyond it stands the Luciferian impulse to destroy reality for my sake, the impatience with the weary burden of creatureliness. Creatureliness means never having 'done with' people or the world or God. It means the risk of response, decision, listening and answering, attending to a constantly shifting environment. (R. Williams, 2005, 42, 43)

With Foucault, the individual as agent has an awesome and burdensome challenge as creator (constructivist) of an entire value universe. The individual self's will to choose, the will to become, and the will to cut oneself off from the world, is truly awesome and frightening.

> Struck by the sense that we stand before a normative abyss, that this blind, deaf, silent universe offers *no* guidance whatever; we can experience an exhilarating challenge, which inspires us, which can even awaken a sense of strange beauty of this alien universe, in the face of which we stake our claim as legislators of meaning. (C. Taylor, 2007, 580-581)

Foucault's project is fascinating, but it fails to pass the rigors of Taylor's criteria for the higher versions of the authentic quest for self-constitution and identity development towards a *thick* self. Taylor proposes that the quest for meaning, and the prospects for a foundation of hope, require that we pay attention to a larger horizon of the good. This he suggests will build sustainability into our fragile moral and spiritual lives. Foucault's philosophy of the aesthetic entails serious vulnerability to loss of meaning and thus we end up back in our prison camp. With Rowan Williams, we want to question the plausibility of the aesthetic moral self.

> We must say No to the temptation to diabolical detachment, the privacy of Satan; and we must learn the patience of attentive love.... To know mourning and pity makes domineering self-assertion unthinkable. Sensitivity to depth and presence of others in their vulnerability rules out bitter and harsh struggle for power in which others are made to pay the price of our fears and insecurities. (R. Williams, 2005, 43, 92)

The next discussion involves a recovery of the moral good. Profound insight emerges into the current attempts to identify and locate ourselves in late modernity, to recover our passion. Another section of the tunnel is complete, and we anticipate that light is coming soon. Yet there is substantial work ahead of us, examining a whole new infrastructure for morality, and recovering the ancient language of the good. We are now moving beyond the confines of our camp. The journey ahead becomes clearer, our resolve stronger.

6

Beyond Nihilism

The Light and Hope of the Hypergood

Foucault offers a minimalist morality focused on freedom, creativity and style. But this has been shown to fall short of what is needed to negotiate late modernity towards a stable identity and a stable society. It increases fragmentation and lands us back in relativism. With Foucault, we will not escape our prison camp of nihilism: beauty (aesthetics) will not save us. But there may indeed be a viable alternative. Can the *good* save us? We find a substantial answer to this question in Canadian philosopher and public intellectual Charles Taylor. His project offers critical help in recovering our passion. It is an approach that brings an important critique to ethical relativism and moral subjectivism. We propose it as a sensitive, fruitful and responsible way forward. Will it get us beyond nihilism and into the light of day?

Taylor's (1989) bold argument for *falsifiable moral realism* is articulated in the first section of his important work *Sources of the Self*. This is a monumental contribution to the recovery and transformation of moral discourse. As he looks at how people reason and deliberate, he argues that, in terms of moral givens, certain perennial features of the self are present irrespective of culture or the way they are expressed or understood. Taylor removes the fear and uncertainty, even the hostility, from moral debate and shows us that we can have sound, rational discourse if we recover the right language. In the long run, we will better understand morality and its diversity with Taylor's help. His offer is substantial and fecund.

He begins with the phenomena of moral experience. The focus is on how humans operate as moral beings, how they reflect upon those experiences and upon the moral behavior of others. He is interested in integration of *praxis* and moral theory, of the immanent and transcendent, the subjective and objective dimensions. Beginning with humans and the way they actually experience and discuss morality, he claims that the most plausible explanation is one that takes seriously one's perception of the *independence* of moral *goods*. This five-fold schema is worthy of serious consideration.

Taylor tends to be more phenomenological. He does not want to substitute a philosophical abstraction for how people live and think morally. Here are the salient features of Taylor's ontology of the good. Firstly, Taylor argues for the ubiquity of moral intuitions and judgments in human experience. These are intuitions that transcend basic human desires for survival, sex, or self-realization. They are referred to as second-order desires, strong evaluations or qualitative discriminations. We highlight the important focus on the qualities of the will. In contrast to Foucault, they must be more than mere choice or self-assertion, or promotion of one's values. This concept of second-order desires appeals to the ancient idea of the good. It is a good that also remains interwoven with the self, but transcends the self in significant ways. This avoids the pitfall of pure subjectivism, which is a real danger in Foucault.

Secondly, he argues that there is a need for a larger moral picture to facilitate the task of making sense of moral experience: debates, deliberations, decisions and actions. He calls this picture or map, a moral *framework* or *horizon*. One can see in this the hermeneutical approach to knowledge. Each framework is made up of several goods held together in a coherent relationship with one another, producing an overarching moral worldview. Certain goods tend to coalesce within the frame. The moral self is in a dialectical relationship with its framework and its constituent goods. The dynamics of this dialectic is what he calls *articulation*. It is not a static set of conditions, but remains dynamic and developmental as we sort through our moral convictions. There is a self-interpretive aspect of one's relationship to the good. The frame affects how individual goods are perceived and how one sees oneself in relation to those goods.

Thirdly, he recognizes that there is a key defining good within each moral framework, which he calls the *hypergood*. The hypergood is the preeminent good and operates as a controlling influence and organizer of the other goods within the framework. It defines its overall character and thus is central to the discussion at hand. Confront another person's hypergood and you will strike something they value deeply, something for which they will fight and give you resistance. The hypergood is a core element in one's moral and spiritual identity.

Fourthly, Taylor recognizes an important narrative (P. Ricoeur, 1992) and communal texture to the pursuit of the good in moral growth. Humans at their best also interpret their lives in narrative and communal terms as they relate to moral goods. These goods give vision, direction and purpose to life. The narrative articulation helps the individual to find a unity amidst the complexity of moral experience and the plurality of goods vying for attention. Sometimes they even conflict, or at the very least, exist in tension. For example, liberty and equality, justice and mercy, efficient success and compassionate understanding can come into conflict, but they are each important moral goods in their own right, claims Taylor. The awareness and cultivation of this narrative and communal dimension is a key factor in the establishment of the meaning of a life, the moral growth of the individual, and one's sense of calling and purpose within a community. People with a strong sense of tradition or cultural heritage understand its significance. Taylor suggests that we do ourselves damage if we do not pay attention to this factor in moral identity.

Fifthly, Taylor speaks of the sources of the moral self, the *constitutive good* (CG). This good, the engine of moral motivation, gives meaning to, and empowers, the hypergood and the other life goods within the moral framework. It acts as a motivator or *moral driver*. The CG is a challenging but highly significant concept. We will unpack it in more detail in Chapter 9. It provides the constitutive ground of the worth or value of the life goods, and empowers the individual to live the good life, to pursue virtue. It takes the discourse beyond mere words and ideals to empower action and healthy moral choice. It speaks to our motivation to *do* and *model* the good. It connects our passion and our *praxis*. CG shows how the good plays out in relationships, how one can embrace a good even when it is costly or causes friction with others. For example, a person might risk the good of their own wellbeing to save a drowning child. In Chapter 9, we will discuss how the Holy Spirit can be a play of this sort of good. When someone has a strong sense of this particular good, they are often in a state of transformation and moral growth. According to Taylor, the CG is something we can also love and admire. It attracts and inspires us, fills us with motivation for life-giving action.

Thus, moral identity, as Taylor sees it in his moral discourse, is interwoven with the pursuit of the good. Contrast this with Foucault's emphasis on freedom and the beautiful. Taylor discerns these five categories as *givens*, structural features that are common to the life of all morally healthy human beings. Sociopaths like Bernie Madoff, who run a fifty billion dollar Ponzi scam, are the exception as they lack empathy and a sense of social accountability. Madoff is morally damaged. Furthermore, these goods are not reducible to mere choice or preference, but they have a transcendent quality to them. They are *innately* or inherently good, whether or not we participate in or embrace them. They are available to empower us as agents who wish to engage the world constructively.

Taylor wants to problematize the occlusion or exclusion of such parameters, such qualitative distinctions for moral reasoning. He believes that there is a multiplicity of goods to be recognized, acted upon, pursued and enjoyed for the benefit of robust human flourishing. They impact how we think, question, talk, carry moral conviction and actually live together in moral space. As a basis for dialogue, they can greatly improve our understanding of one another.

Taylor offers a moral ontology of the self at its best, noblest or most whole and we believe that he has every right to do so. It retrieves key concepts that have been buried by recent moral discourse, which has been narrowed far too much. It makes it possible for a moral debate that is a healthy, rational enterprise. We can talk sensibly and winsomely about the goods that drive our world or that of others. It also provides a rational mechanism to sort out moral differences in a fair, civil, and understanding way. One way to learn about our dialogue partner or friend, even our enemy, from a different context, religion, culture or country is to ask strategic questions concerning their passion about personal, moral or cultural goods and priorities. In the interest of building fruitful dialogue, some questions are offered at the end of this chapter.

On the basis of Taylor's moral plausibility structure, we mount our critique of the idea that freedom can be reduced to matter of the will alone, or naked, unqualified, self-justifying individual choice—the stance of nihilism. That position is highly suspect and contestable. Choice or will is only one small dimension of the moral self and must be seen in its larger context and complexity. There is a complexity of having so many goods. The conflicts between some of them emerge at certain moments in life, but this complexity is what we have to negotiate in the quest for our own flourishing. Taylor cautions us to keep the various goods in play, not to bury or disparage them just because there is a situational rivalry between them. Some moral philosophers have reduced their theory to one of the goods, such as personal happiness (*eudaemonia*). Life brings these conflicts into play and that makes it interesting and challenging. But these goods prevent it from becoming defeatist, or skewed. Sometimes one has to sacrifice one good for another temporarily, towards the greater good or a superior outcome. This takes hard reflection.

Next, we explore the details and character of the hypergood. According to this brilliant thinker, the potential resolution of the dilemma of the plurality of goods, or the tension between goods, comes by way of a highest good among the *strongly-valued* goods. One can actually gain wisdom from the tension between certain goods. Within the moral framework, this is called the 'hypergood' (C. Taylor, 1989, 63-73, 100-102, 104-106). Taylor summarizes his insight.

> Let me call higher-order goods of this kind 'hypergoods', i.e. goods which are incomparably more important than the others, but provide the standpoint from which these [other goods] must be weighed, judged, decided about." (C. Taylor, 1989, 63)

The hypergood has hierarchical priority or preeminence, as it also has a significant control and shaping power within the moral framework. It is the highest ideal, of which the self is most conscious, most passionate, a good that rests at the very core of one's being. It shapes our identity. Challenge this good and you will touch a moral nerve cord, a person's moral deep structure. Find this good in another, and you will know something precious about them. People bond around their hypergood, join partnerships, form NGOs or marry based on a common hypergood. Become aware of this good in yourself, and you will be in touch with your deepest passion and sense of calling. Many college students are instinctively searching for such a good as they seek to develop their passion.

The hypergood effectively orchestrates the arrangement and hierarchy of other goods. It interprets their priority and adjusts their moral play. It can raise or lower their priority, promote or demote them, sort them out when they come in conflict, or even eliminate certain goods from moral play altogether.

For example, the pleasure and convenience of driving a car can be put aside for the sake of saving the biosphere, or environmental stewardship. One can ride a bicycle or take public transportation to work. Is this not the purpose of a mission statement, to rally around a hypergood? We carefully attend to this moral driver in groups or institutions with which we associate, especially the company where we work. It is vital that the individual be very conscious of, and well positioned with respect to this particular good in order to keep their integrity. This *preeminent good* grounds and directs one's overall moral beliefs, goals, and aspirations. It works to define and give important shape to one's entire life. One could accurately say that it rests at the spiritual center of one's personality and gives deep meaning to one's very existence. One could honestly say, "I know who I am and where I stand, because I am in touch with my central driver, my hypergood."

Examples of the hypergood (C. Taylor, 1989, p. 65) given by Taylor are happiness, equal respect, universal justice, divine will, self-respect and self-fulfillment. One could easily imagine a family, clan or country, or the health of the biosphere being such a hypergood. There can be conflict between these hypergoods as well, which leads to public, personal and international controversies and strong differences of opinion on testy matters. Wisdom requires a sophisticated understanding of the goods at play in any negotiation. For example, when John F. Kennedy was negotiating with Nikita Krushchev during the Cuban Missile Crisis, he had to pay close attention to what goods were at stake for the Soviets (American nuclear missiles in Turkey).

One can easily see this conflict happening among the three major hypergoods in Western culture: (a) universal justice and reduction of human suffering (concern for the victim), (b) self-determining, self-expressive freedom, and (c) the hypergood of affirmation of everyday life or equal respect. Because of these, we end up with various priorities and political tensions, but with this concept, we can come to understand what is at stake in these tensions, draw out what is hidden beneath the surface. Perhaps then we are less threatened by a particular political play or we can explain our political views better. *Agape* love is one hypergood that Taylor thinks we cannot exclude out of hand because it has shaped so many in the West and now around the world. In Chapter 8, we unpack the power of this hypergood in much more detail. The value added in the discernment of hypergoods is the ability to understand what is at stake in a difference of opinion or controversy. It allows one to actively apply wisdom, avoid offence and bring healing and peace to relationships by negotiating between such goods.

This good has a major influence on how an individual's moral horizon is articulated, the hierarchy of life goods and how one is generally oriented in moral space. The powerful hypergood is independent, and shapes the desires and choices of lesser goods. It is not merely an ideal or the mere object of a high admiration or contemplation (a mere poetic entity). The hypergood can be quite demanding on the self, and often requires great personal sacrifice. Examples include civil disobedience by laying down your body in front of logging trucks to save an old growth forest, risking arrest to identify with an oppressed minority as in the Civil Rights movement. It could involve reporting on a war and its victims at risk of one's personal safety, chaining oneself to a nuclear submarine to fight for peace and stop the arms race. Another might leave the comfort of a classroom or academic post to work on the streets of Calcutta with those who are most marginalized. It is the case that the greater the sacrifice the deeper is the identification with one's hypergood.

What is the actual role of the hypergood in moral self-constitution? What is one's possible relationship to this particular good? How does it impact one's identity? According to Taylor, a self with the requisite depth and complexity to have an identity—a *thick* self–must be defined in terms of such a good. One's life is interwoven with it. Taylor (1989, 63) notes that, "It is orientation to this which comes closest to defining my identity, and therefore my direction to this good is of unique importance to me." It provides the marker against which the individual measures her direction and progress in life. The stronger the influence of the hypergood, the more integrated and trustworthy the individual becomes—we can say we know this person. Merely dabbling in an eclectic pool of currently available values or moral trendiness is not enough for a substantial, sustainable self.

Finally, we grow towards such a good because it is something that motivates us deeply, providing an emotional and spiritual center. Taylor (1989, 73) says significantly, "Our acceptance of any hypergood is connected in a complex way with our being *moved* by it." His nuanced and compelling claim is that this is not only a phenomenological account of some individual selves, but an exploration of the very limits of the conceivable, an anthropological *given*.

> To know who I am is a species of knowing where I stand. My identity is defined by the commitments and identifications which provide the frame or horizon within which I try to decide from case to case what is good, or valuable, or what ought to be done or what I endorse or oppose ... It is the horizon within which I am capable of taking a stand ... It is to be oriented in moral space, a space in which questions arise about what is good or bad, what is worth doing and what not, what has meaning and importance for you and what is trivial and secondary. (C. Taylor, 1989, 27, 28)

It can help a cynical, morally confused person to heal from nihilism, to grow in confidence, with a strong sense of direction.

Taylor helps clear the fog and confusion around pluralism versus plurality. Profoundly, he suggests that the hypergood could include the fulfillment of one's duties, obligations and responsibilities to and for others. This is a thought attentive to the important work of French philosopher Emmanuel Lévinas, who recognizes the social aspect of identity as one's sense of obligation and responsibility *in the face of the other.* It is a stark contrast to the radical stance of anarchy.

> Responsibility for the Other transports the self beyond the sphere of self-interest. Other-responsibility could also be seen as the greatest form of self-realization, featuring as the highest vocation of human subjectivity (C. Taylor, 1989, 112).

As a hypergood, *other-responsibility* can be integrated into the structure of selfhood without compromising the exteriority of the claims of the other. This is foundational to empathy and compassion, the give and take of most relationships, to healthy covenants, and ultimately to the quest for the common good. One of the weaknesses of Foucault's ethics is that he poses ethics as a contest, based in an ideological use of freedom as an *agonisme* or resistance. This is very one-sided and self-centered.

But our resistance in the escape from nihilism is against narrow self-interest and entitlement, and for the sake of the common good Social reformer Jim Wallis operates in the same orbit as Taylor.

> Here is the road for an era of moral economy: from massive inequality to decent equity; from the narrow definition of shareholders to a broader vision of stakeholders; from short-term to long-term thinking and acting; from the ethics of endless growth to the ethics of sustainability; from doing well to also doing good; and from broken social contracts to a new social covenant between citizens, business and government.... Let's look at what it would mean to start moving toward a more moral economy that could enhance rather than undermine the common good. (J. Wallis, 2014, 201)

That changes everything. Wallis, who has much to say with integrity on the common good, offers substantial hope for American political life and democracy in general. His instincts help us tunnel out of nihilism into the light of day. It does seem that, as a culture, we have disconnected rights from the language of the common good. Perhaps it is time for a renewal of Taylor's nuanced discourse on the good to balance some of the most perverse and distorted emendations of rights language usage: those which are consumeristic, narcissistic and individualistic. We dare not lose rights language, but we definitely need to renew the horizon within which it is articulated—reconnecting rights to virtue, community, memory and the good.

> Redeeming democracy for the sake of the common good will require several things: turning consumers into citizens, widening political involvement, confronting the greed and power that subvert democracy, and overcoming the final barrier to democracy: the control of money over politics. Only those major commitments can turn political isolation into participation, take us from polarization to progress, and move us from paralysis to solutions.... We now see citizens engaging in community organizing and mobilizing around public issues that take them beyond narrow electoral goals and into a whole new world of making our life together better. (J. Wallis, 2014, 185)

In order to deepen and ground this discourse of the good, we extend our quest to the larger horizon of the transcendent. In this trajectory, we ascend above radical skepticism that can emerge within radical individual choice theory. We are willing to work hard and search our history in search of a richer moral horizon. It is one that leads to an exploration of the connection between human goods and divine goodness—something lost during various stages of modernity. We are beginning to see some light at the end of the tunnel. Things are set up for a fruitful quest toward moral empowerment and renewal. But first, we need to discuss some important issues around the recovery of language itself in Chapter 7. This provides an important bridge to a transcendent turn to *agape* love in Chapter 8.

Below are some provocative questions to help us dialogue about the goods carried by other people or other *tribes*. This can promote discussion of the good in various spheres. The whole dialogue ought to be seeded with curiosity, respect and sensitive appreciation. It is vulnerable to speak of these things, so we must bring our best sensitivity to the table. The goal is to fathom the cherished beliefs of our dialogue partner. If we take the posture of an investigative journalist, we can discern the drivers that influence our friends and colleagues. This posture will show respect, and assist in connection and communication. Popular blogger and author Seth Godin says that we presently live in a *connection economy*. It is all about taking leadership in building trust and openness, showing genuine interest, coming from an openness to be mutually teachable. This can provide solid ground for healthy dialogue for students or people within a neighborhood, between spouses, within an institution, charity or business. It will move us into active engagement that takes responsibility for how people think, rational and irrational, while we call each other to a higher moral standard. Bestselling author David Brooks (2015, 262-267) offers an excellent book of stories on character development within the drama of real life. The Humility Code at the end of the book is very revealing, instructive of how the language of the good applies to our moral growth, economy and identity.

Ten Dynamic Questions about Identity and the Moral Good

1. What do you perceive as the central driving aspirations of people?
2. Do you think people are interested in dialogue about the common good or are they only committed to their own self-interest? What good(s), virtue, or character trait are you passionate about?
3. Where do you see yourself moving philosophically: new convictions, deconstruction of past beliefs, disillusioned, hopeful, passionate?
4. What gives your life hope, meaning and direction?

5. What figure or author has most profoundly influenced and inspired you? Which individual in David Brooks' *The Road to Character* most inspires you and why? What public figure has most disillusioned you and why?

6. What do you think makes people cynical about noble values and strong character? Where is this current malaise in our society sourced?

7. What promotes human flourishing? Is it pursuit of individual freedom or some empathic contribution to another human being, some good or higher goal? Is there a transcendent dimension beyond survival (safety, food, medicine, education) that contributes to our flourishing?

8. Are there important human questions that science cannot ask and should not try to ask? Do such questions around the topic of meaning, identity, and moral drivers still have currency?

9. Do you think it is important to ask some of the Big Life Questions and think through personal beliefs and convictions about them?

10. Do you have a sense of your moral framework or your hypergood? Is God or *agape* love part of that framework in any way? What stories, books, authors feed your moral and spiritual imagination?

7

Beyond Nihilism

Recovering the Power of Word amidst the Language Games

Language is essential for dialogue across plural views of life lived well. It helps us find just and harmonious ways to live together on planet earth amidst an increasing speed of change. But there is also a sense in which we need to recover language in its fullness, like the ancient language of the good, as part of our escape from nihilism. Language must be seen in terms of its rich embedding and deeper context. Language allows us to communicate, and summons us to the table of critical conversation. We are fallible and diverse, but nonetheless language allows us to unite in the search for the truth, to explore the broader horizon of meaning, making sense of it all. We must never give up this quest, however difficult it seems at times. The larger horizon of our reason gives it fecundity, bold imagination, and keeps it from dying a slow death. Language offers us a tool to share our best wisdom across time, tradition and national boundaries. It allows us to debate issues of common concern. Philosophically, we have made the *linguistic turn* in the twentieth century. Through language, we inevitably shape our world, and are shaped by words and grammar, the salient articulation.

Creation is a language all its own, as we experience in watching the sunrise over a calm lake with a lonely loon passing in the mist. We sense a presence and a peace that runs deep. The beauty of the Canadian Rockies or the majesty of the Grand Canyon shouts with speech that almost cuts us. Language is the foundation of biological life as we see in the semiotics of our very DNA—an amazing 3.5 billion base pairs of code. Snowfields and glaciers grasp reality in a speech that empowers our spirit. Tropical canopies are a poem of complexity, unity with incredible diversity of life. The universe speaks volumes with its billions of galaxies and stars that put us in our place. Who can fathom 13.8 billion light years of cosmic development? Language is a means of seeing as well as hearing.

Text is a key focal point of attention in late modernity. Nietzsche tells us that. Students in the arts, humanities and social sciences think a lot about language: sign, signifier, and signified. What will enhance the capacity of their grammar, and rhetorical skill, their articulate grasp of a subject? We envy the great poets like T.S. Eliot, E.E. Cummings, or playwrights like Shakespeare who possess iconic skill in word craft and *poesis*. We long to be the powerful storyteller like Pulitzer Prize winner Marilynne Robinson. We desperately want to find our voice, to communicate our passion to the world. We also love to learn the art of deconstruction, to expose deceptive power interests and dark motives hidden in writing, sales pitches, obfuscation or nefarious political rhetoric. There is also the amazing and significant world of our body language, with its multiple non-verbal cues. The power of word is palpable.

Immigrants quickly realize that they are quite vulnerable without competence in the language of their new homeland. They feel lost and powerless, often marginal. Many are tasked with the challenge to master the new language, but left alone they revert back to the safety of their tongue of origin. We are indeed *homo linguisticus* (the language animal). What university graduate is not amazed by the many worlds they have explored through language? Language renders life intense and interesting. Our best interlocutors offer us wisdom and hope, speaking into our lives.

Academics collect millions of words, analyze them, compare them, translate and decipher ancient scripts. Libraries brim with millions of books, journals and periodicals, digital articles. Google is making so much more information available to everyone with an Internet connection or access to a cyber café. The final dissertation in one's PhD needs to be very carefully written, often taking months or years to complete, to get the language and grammar just right. We write, think, and edit incessantly. We make a close reading of the text in order to have credibility in our analytical work.

Academics also deconstruct the language of those whose perspective they oppose, or a previous regnant philosophical regime they wish to depose. Late modern thinkers deconstruct early modern views in order to reconstruct new perspectives, as Foucault did with the concept of the self. Sometimes, however, we can trivialize language by reducing it to mere sophist games that get played at academic seminars or colloquia, and especially late night discussions in the dorm. Words, signs and symbols are a hot commodity, a major currency of universities in all fields. Students cut their teeth on the language of their discipline. If we transfer fields, a whole new intimidating vocabulary awaits us. Lawyers make their living with language, logic, sound argument and good grammar, the poignant question. It can mean life or death, success or failure in a court case. Wording is critical in a merger contract, dispute resolution, criminal defense or a peace agreement. A national constitution or charters of rights and freedoms is a powerful use of language.

Much ink has been spilt in recent years on the role of discourse as a source of the self. Identity is deeply embedded in language, which in turn helps to constitute the self. We all have a vital relationship with our mother tongue where we first found meaning, where we learn to use language to accomplish endeavors, find nurture and engage others. Language is our existential lifeline. Like we breathe air, we think and speak words to make sense of the world. To articulate is to flourish. From our earliest days, we are involved in the wonderful art of articulation, making the tacit more explicit, finding the words that resonate with us, with *reality* as we know it. It is this process whereby the aspects of the world are identified, clarified and made accessible. Consequently, they can empower us in both speech and action. The individual self emerges amidst an ongoing culture-shaping conversation in some specific life-world. The language game is already in motion when we arrive on the scene.

Humanities scholar Crystal Downing (2006) among many others shows the importance of language in interpreting the late modern self. She notes a two-way dialectic phenomenon between self and language. Self is neither totally transcendent of language (early modern tendency), nor a mere product or effect of language (late modern tendency). Things are more complex. As noted Boston College sociologist Peter Berger points out, there is a sense in which humans make the world and the world in turn shapes them and their descendants (P. Berger and T. Luckmann, 1967, *The Social Construction of Reality*). We both inherit and contribute to our linguistic heritage. We both interpret, and are in turn interpreted, through language. We self-interpret and learn about ourselves through self-articulation. Andy Crouch in his clever work *Culture Making* (2008) writes that we are meaning makers, that culture is, to a large extent, us trying to make sense of the world.

> Making sense of the wonder and terror of the world is the original human preoccupation. And it is this deeper sense of culture that most clearly distinguishes us from the rest of creation.... We simply have no indication that any other creature wonders about the mystery of the world. (A. Crouch, 2008, 24)

We try to pick up the theme, the tone of the conversation, as quickly as we are able, to get into what philosopher Ludwig Wittgenstein calls the *language game*. This is why we spend so much of our early years in school. It is foundational for *homo lingisticus*. The alternative is a painful and frightening alienation—sitting alone on the sidelines. Life and public discourse go on without us, and we lose everything. We cannot engage society, the law, economic exchange, or political theatre without good language. Linguistic autism is terrifying. Political leaders look for the language that resonates with the people they are trying to impress, sometimes employing power words (freedom, equality, change, hope) to gain public resonance and win precious votes. They promote a dream and promise the world. Perhaps it is more common than we think to become speechless, especially when we step outside the confines of our discipline or culture of birth. To misunderstand language, to be unable to communicate, is to be alone, powerless to understand the world, vulnerable to exploitation and abuse. We strategically map or come to understand our reality, our discipline, and master our skill set through language.

But sometimes there is too much emphasis on language as an end in itself, as the ultimate thing, or the only important thing. The tool can become the tyrant. How can we avoid the *gnosticism* of settling only for the intra-linguistic (signs indicating signs), which leaves language disconnected to anything outside itself—separation of signifier from signified, separation of word from world? One famous author just stopped writing for an entire year because of this frustration. For him, the blank page was a sign of this disconnect between word and world, and therefore he wanted to highlight its futility. Why write at all if it is mere words about words, sentences within sentences like a labyrinth, going nowhere, making no difference? Wheaton College English Professor Roger Lundin (1993, *Culture of Interpretation*) effectively describes this condition where language is reified and the self is repressed and demoted to become its victim. There are times and circumstances when language can become our nemesis and we its prisoners. The content and connotation of language is critical. For example, words like 'freedom' or 'choice' or 'creativity' or 'difference' are loaded with various conflicting and contestable meanings, dependent on context, intent and author, and the conversational players at hand.

In solidarity with Plato, we want to avoid inauthentic sophist rhetoric, mere argument for its own sake, cynicism about truth and integrity, an exercise of the lungs only. Things can get a bit confusing, and even implode into cynicism: *dissolution*. This is where we think we have lost the center of it all, the connection with a core 'reality'. Distinguished University of Virginia sociologist James Davison Hunter (2010) writes incisively about the daunting problem of *dissolution* as a key aspect of nihilism, and a crisis of language.

> The modern world, by its very nature, questions if not negates the trust that connects human discourse and the "reality" of the world. In its mildest expressions, it questions the adequacy of language to make the world intelligible. In its more aggressive expressions, however, it fosters a doubt that what is said has anything to do with what exists "out there".... The problem is this: when the objectified and shared meaning of words are undermined, when we no longer have confidence that words signify what we thought they signified, then it is possible to impute any meaning to words one desires. If words can mean anything, then they have no intrinsic meaning or at least no possibility of a common meaning. They only mean what we say.... None make any sense outside their own specific discourse.... In a culture in which the covenant between signified and signifier, word and world is broken, words are emptied of meaning. The forces of dissolution, then, lead us to a place of absence, a place where we can never be confident of what is real, what is true, what is good.... The only thing left to connect words to the world are will and power—that is a will to power rooted in desires and judgments that have no justification but are their own measure of moral worth and significance. (J.D. Hunter, 2010, 205-6)

This is a big concern today and not easily resolved. As we have seen in the last two chapters, Foucault claims that ethics is an art of individual expression and a product of our will and our creativity, while Taylor says ethics is our relationship with the good in community, part of a story that makes sense of our lives. These identity paradigms are in opposition and tension in culture today. They employ a different language, with the term ethics meaning something quite different to each philosopher. How do we discern the situation, and avoid a nihilistic dead end, a linguistic and moral autism? How does language actually work constructively, genuinely, and faithfully to unite us in common cause and mutual understanding?

Let us explore another relationship between self and language. This is critical for anyone's identity formation because language is a heavyweight in shaping us morally, spiritually and intellectually. Language can make us more *human*. We often do not recognize this until we leave home the first time or exit the cocoon of our undergraduate program, and take a new job in our first very intense language context—where understanding the cultural language of the boss matters immensely. Brilliant UK hermeneutics philosopher and theologian Anthony Thiselton (1995) agrees that the dynamics of self and language, self and text, are much richer and more complex than sometimes understood. But he wisely rejects the idea of incommensurability between language games. He believes in an *integral plurality*, a deeper unity amidst the diversity of cultures. Otherwise, we would lose the ability to dialogue about vital matters at the United Nations or the International Criminal Court.

Although most great religions make universal claims, Yale scholar Miraslov Volf (2015, 93) believes that there is a basis for friendly dialogue between them, if willing epistemological humility is in play. He and others have made significant progress in dialogue between Christianity and Islam in particular with the *A Common Word* document, signed by many top scholars. He clearly shows that it is possible to learn from different religious and ideological perspectives, to recognize both their similarities and differences, without imploding into mindless cultural or moral relativism or culture wars. There is an acute need to realize that other religions desire to contribute to human flourishing as well. If they apply the religious virtue of hospitality in a positive ethos of generosity of spirit, there can be a creative engagement and mutual learning. These faiths have potential for contributing to global conflict resolution—to mitigate negative forces. Religion should always be a voice resisting oppression and injustice in the larger conversation of mankind. Professor Volf is joined in this sentiment by peacemaker and public intellectual Rabbi Jonathan Sacks (2002, *Dignity of Difference*), former Chief Rabbi of the United Hebrew Congregations of the Commonwealth. They mean to contribute a key piece of the puzzle to help us find our place and passion in late modernity. They want to help mitigate the clash of civilizations and to encourage mutual understanding of narratives. The right language and careful understanding is vital to this task.

Charles Taylor offers some expertise on the philosophy of language (1989, 35-41). He writes that: "To study persons is to study beings who only exist in, or are partly constituted by a certain language". He is also sensitive to two quite different uses of language, two linguistic paradigms: expressive and designative. Taylor is capable in both kinds of language game and critical of certain aspects of each language tradition. See also Alasdair McIntyre (1990), *Three Rival Versions of Moral Inquiry: Encyclopedia, Genealogy and Tradition* for a masterful presentation of three different articulations of identity and morality.

a. Expressivist-Constitutive Language Usage (Herder, Hamann, Humboldt, Gadamer)

In this culture, we recognize that metaphysics cannot be done by abstracting from language, but by turning to it. It recognizes the mystery that surrounds language. Truth does not look for the conditions by which language refers to reality; instead truth is manifest through music, art, facial expressions, liturgy, the aesthetic. Sentences are much too limiting to be the primary vehicles bearing the weight of truth. This tradition draws on a more Augustinian understanding of language. Everything is a sign.

Charles Taylor places the later Wittgenstein in this tradition (while the earlier Wittgenstein fits in the designative tradition). This tradition avoids a crude *instrumentalization* of language as the basis for truth. Wittgenstein actually went through a philosophical conversion and changed traditions mid-career. We tend to see this use of language in Continental European philosophy. Humanities scholar Jens Zimmermann has a keen grasp of this tradition (*The Passionate Intellect* 2006; *Incarnational Humanism* 2012a; *Hermeneutics: A Very Short Introduction*, 2015). It is operative in cultural studies, the humanities, education, some aspects of social sciences, and the arts. The focus tends to be on how we live, our human social location. It is generally more open to the transcendent, although not always.

b. Designative Language Usage (Hobbes, Locke, Condillac)

In this culture, we trap the pursuit of wisdom within language and confine it to immanence, where language and its relationship to truth are reduced to pointing. It is more flattened. Language primarily designates objects in the world. The object is observed but not participated in. One assumes a use of language based on *quantitative* judgments that are non-subject dependent. This tradition contributes to a mechanistic universe, leaving it *disenchanted* with respect to higher meaning. It is committed to the primacy of epistemology (evidence and justified belief). It is not oriented to universals or essences, but is more empirical in its approach and emphasis. We tend to find this usage in the hard sciences and social sciences or where ideological scientism is applied to other disciplines. Its use is more dominant in Anglo-American or Analytical philosophy.

Taylor goes on to highlight the communitarian aspects of language within the expressive-constitutive usage. This insight is very important for us as we proceed to transcend or move beyond the confines of nihilism. We find accountability and nurture in conversation, within our narrative, within a community of speakers, showing the key public aspect of language. We dig deep in order to find the right words to express our convictions. Taylor summarizes it well:

> The question 'who?' places someone as an interlocutor in a society of interlocutors (conversation partners).... A language only exists and is maintained within a linguistic community. Therefore, a self is only a self among other selves. A self can never be described without reference to those who surround it .... I define who I am by defining where I speak from, in the family tree, in social space, in the geography of social statuses and functions, in my intimate relations to the ones I love, and also crucially in the space of moral and spiritual orientation within which my most important defining relations are lived out.... Because language is never private, it serves to place some matter out in the open between interlocutors...to put things in public space. The constitutive dimension of language provides the medium through which some of our most important concerns, the characteristically human concerns, can impinge on us all. This makes possible judgments and standards. (C. Taylor, 1989, 28, 35 and 239).

Within academia, we are much better positioned if we find the right community of good, wise and witty interlocutors, excellence in mentorship, the cutting edge school of thought in our field. Of course, we cannot all be from top ranked schools, but we are often willing to traverse oceans or continents to find conversation with the right people, especially for a PhD or Postdoctoral Fellowship. Because this offers us a more refined language community, it is urgent that we seek out wise conversation, in order to get the most out of our educational experience. We become sophisticated, aware of the linguistic movers and shakers who shape the field, and sometimes we are tempted to venerate them, because they enhance our identity. Even outside our field, and even if we disagree with them, they become the markers against which we identify our position. We frequent their offices and rub shoulders at conferences with the prescient, cutting edge thinkers, the trusted and respected people of deep insight and noble character. They are masters of their domain. This whole process shapes us in significant ways.

A language community is both intensive and extensive. We must also beware of too narrow a base of interlocutors, which can make us myopic, narrow and brittle, even dogmatic. Eventually, we will enter a working community where there is another language group that will require us to adapt. Our conversation with the ancients, the Greeks, Romans, the biblical authors, key literati, other great minds, moral exemplars, early church fathers or other historical figures offers us a great gift to our identity and our linguistic skill set. We late moderns did not arrive from another planet fully formed, but have a important cultural and linguistic history. Many of the rich conversations in which we participate began centuries ago. If we become too narrow in our interests, we could be depriving ourselves intellectually, and stifling our creativity. Early Modern European history professor Brad Gregory (2012) from Notre Dame notes: "We cannot understand the character of contemporary realities until and unless we see how they have been shaped and are still being shaped by the distant past." Historical memory is important. As with Taylor, his scholarship covers major changes in perspective in Western thought that have occurred over half a millennium. Both have tremendous insights to offer us, tracing changes in the use of language over these five centuries.

Peter Harrison (1998), Andreas Idreos Professor of Science and Religion at the University of Oxford, is also a prime interlocutor on the history and philosophy of science, especially the influence of faith on the emergence of science. He confronts what Taylor has called the *subtraction theory* of science and religion, demonstrating through historical perspective that Christianity was a vital and necessary inspiration to the rise of science. Far from being a detriment to scientific exploration, a number of scholars have pointed out that it was precisely Christian theological concepts–and especially those that emerged during the Protestant

Reformation–that propelled empirical investigation of nature. So science was not a way to lose one's faith. It was Christian faith that compelled scientific exploration, that provided its infrastructure. We shouldn't simply confuse the history of science with the rise of philosophical naturalism. Harrison deftly shows how it was a shift in biblical hermeneutics that gave rise to a very different way of "reading" nature that we now associate with the scientific method. Noted biophysicist and university provost Tom McLeish (2014) of Durham University agrees. Such scholars share with us a linguistic and cultural heritage, enrich our language base, and correct our popular misconceptions. Dr. McLeish is a champion of creative interdisciplinary dialogue. Others, like noted philosopher Alvin Plantinga (2012), challenge certain versions of contemporary worldview arrogance and prejudice, by pressing the New Atheist rhetoric to the standard of critical scrutiny.

Both the church and university are significant carriers of heritage, intellectual tradition and human understanding. At times in history, the church was the university; there was no higher learning outside the purview of the church. Societies need religion as well as academic insights from across the disciplines for accountability, change and progress. They offer us intelligence that both complement and correct each other. Sometimes they conflict, but there is also substantial agreement. Religion brings us into creative connection with that which we can neither control, fully know or master, and that element is good for discovery and learning. There is a bonding, a relatedness and attentiveness to a realm of goodness that is beyond human appropriation, manipulation or control. Indeed, we stand on the shoulders of giants and we should appreciate those shoulders and their sources of wisdom. For wisdom is what we all seek at our best no matter the discipline.

Hermeneutics shows us that a game has been in progress, and that we are entering a discourse, a conversation already in play. We would strongly challenge today's students to learn the various language games that flourish. This is a good word for interdisciplinary study or liberal arts education as a strong foundation to any discipline and source of creativity in science, law, medicine, business, politics and other areas of scholarship. At the very least, we would benefit from coming to understand the philosophical history of our major subject. One of the great opportunities of graduate school is to enrich our linguistic grasp of reality, to become aware of the different voices impacting culture, both within and beyond our discipline. It has been the author's privilege to expand his personal horizons by study in the medical sciences, humanities, cultural studies and theology. Curiosity keeps one on a growing edge. In the Graduate and Faculty Christian Forum at University of British Columbia, it has been our privilege to explore great insights and questions from scholars across the academic spectrum and from top universities around the globe. We have been able to explore the big questions and debate cutting edge, sometimes controversial, issues in a congenial atmosphere.

What is the way of wisdom, the way forward, once we have tunneled to freedom from our nihilist confinement? Academia to some extent is a conversation with the *grands pensées* (great minds) of the past and present. We need these intellectual godfathers and godmothers on our team. Our fellow interlocutors are also crucial to our ongoing grasp of self-understanding and self-discovery—part of this *offering of uncles*. It does not mean that we always have to agree with them, but they make us more human, add more depth and dimensionality to our experience, expand our intellectual horizons, and challenge our prejudices. Taylor warns us that to leave all interlocution communities is to attempt to leap out of the human condition and completely reinvent oneself. This is most dangerous, leading to intellectual poverty and possibly psychic break. With this richer historical understanding, we can see through the smoke and mirrors of current deception, fake rhetoric and clever intellectual obfuscation. Such an ancient virtue was once called *prudence*.

Now more than ever, we also need to include the global conversation partners such as the research team of Al Gore (*The Future: six drivers of global change*, 2012); and Miraslov Volf (*Flourishing: why we need religion on a globalized world*, 2015). Furthermore, we have the valuable work of think tanks like Brookings Institution, Munk School of Global Affairs at University of Toronto, Liu Institute for Global Issues at UBC. We have the current challenge of becoming global citizens, sometimes mastering two or three languages. To be educated today, means getting involved in these global concerns as well. We need to attend to the negative side effects of globalization: the inequities, environmental challenges, consumerism, and exploitation, the failure to address widespread poverty and disease, the insensitivity to local tradition, cultures, and the spiritual poverty of unlimited pursuit of wealth. We live amidst tectonic pressures of contemporary global forces: climate change, militarism and nationalism, refugee crises, terrorism wars, economic inequity, oppression of women. Too often governments allow security and power to trump ethics and religion, making control and innovative military technology their highest priority. This is clearly out of balance and unwise. People like Gore, Volf, Wallis and Sacks have shown us the bigger picture on the human story, with a sense of call to peace, justice and responsibility for the common good.

The Vertical Dimension of Language

There is a meta-dimension to language, a deeper, richer, and higher reality that helps us *see* more clearly, listen more carefully. It is critical to human social and intellectual flourishing. We will show this as *strong* transcendence. Language articulates a way of seeing and thinking, an outlook, and is never free from some kind of metaphysics, as we have seen, even for atheism. British intellectual John Milbank claims that we end up adopting either religion or nihilism, that secular (exclusive or scientific) humanism is very problematic, self-disintegrating and internally contradictory. It is ungrounded. Science was never designed to be a worldview or the ground for a vision of living as a human being. Many great thinkers, along with Charles Taylor, do not buy the thesis of secularity that involves the subtraction theory of religion: the disenchantment view: as science grows, religion is reduced or replaced. For example, Durham University Biophysicist Tom McLeish sums it up well in this more reflective, humble view of science.

> We know better than to swallow an inadequate narrative that portrays science as simply replacing an ancient world of myth and superstition with a modern one of fact and comprehension.... Science is the love of wisdom of natural things.... Its primary creative grammar is the question rather than the answer. Its primary energy is imagination rather than fact. Its primary experience is more typically trial rather than triumph—the journey of understanding already travelled always appears to be a trivial distance compared with the mountain road ahead. (T. McLeish, 2014, 102)

The experience of last centuries two world wars, the Holocaust, the arms race and other attempts at genocide reveal the limitations of a *disenchantment* outlook. We clearly need wisdom, a *quality* of the will, beyond what is provided by science and technology. It is good to remember that science (natural philosophy) began as the search for wisdom about natural things, as McLeish (2014) articulates so well in his book *Faith and Wisdom in Science*.

Charles Taylor is aware of the *transcendent condition* of our having a grasp of our own language, especially as we explore the *expressive-poetic* tradition. We often discover this phenomenon in dialogue (C. Taylor, 1989, 37). In order to progress in our discussion of identity formation and our freedom, we suggest that a return to transcendence is central to the recovery of language from its flatness and deadness. The ability to name things in their depth of meaning as George Steiner notes (*Real Presences,* 1991) must be recovered. It means that we are able to step beyond our own place and agenda, to understand ourselves, and others, as playing a part in the larger whole. This allows for the development of common space, a *polis*. As Taylor puts it, "Some of the most crucial human fulfillments are not possible even in principle for a sole human being.... Our sense of good and sense of self are deeply interwoven and they connect with the way we are agents who share a language with other agents" (C. Taylor, 1989, 40, 41). We know how good this feels when we genuinely commune and connect with others, when there is a robust engagement with other minds. It is a rich pleasure.

Taylor notes that the contemporary quest for meaning, identity or fullness can be met by building something into one's life, some pattern of higher action or excellence, a connection with the good. In the next chapter, we discuss such a fruitful connection with *agape* love. This is one serious and definitive path upward, out of nihilism, opening a new horizon. It can be met by connecting one's life with some greater reality or larger story (C. Taylor, 1989, 46). Ultimately for the believer in *agape* love, one's conversation with God and his saints brings into play this transcendence of identity, this larger horizon of meaning. Ergo, one is using language in a very fruitful and positive way, a richer, even a healing way. Many would agree that there is a deep need for healing in our Western narrative. *Agape* love taps into a special life-giving heritage, which gives perspective on the struggles of the present, connecting collective memory with present and future thinking.

Strong transcendence (Calvin Schrag, 1997) means we are becoming something *more,* better persons, not just new and different, or bizarre. We are reaching out for higher, deeper, richer, nobler aspirations. Identity formation is also about using language to self-interpret, to articulate, define and discover self. We must constantly answer the question, "Who am I and what do I stand for and what am I able to contribute?" This is an important implication of the sociality of the self, forwarded by Taylor (1989, 34). Contrary to the traditional view in certain sectors of academia, the self is not an object or substance in the usually understood sense. We are not selves in the way we are organisms and we don't have selves in the way we have livers and lungs. As Taylor points out, it is a fundamentally misguided question to ask what a person is in abstraction from his or her own self-interpretation. This dynamic self-interpretation is worked out in community through a language conversation and a story, a commitment to the good and to the common good. It helps an individual know where they stand, and how they are accepted as a valid articulation of various identity questions and orientation within society. These identity questions are delicate and vital to everyone, not just minorities. It may take many a walk on the beach or hike to sort through things.

With this richer understanding of language, there emerges a fullness of self within a social space, a self that is conscious of, and in congruity with, narrative and personal history. This is extremely hopeful for late moderns, full of prospects for personal growth and change. Now we are able to explore the concept of *agape* love as one very rich and powerful language that we would do well to recover as a moral compass for late modernity. It is a weighty, substantial postulate. We are now out of the camp, beyond nihilism and cynicism, exploring new horizons of identity and engagement, attentive to new dimensions of reality, with new maps and a compass.

Language is a *gift* to humans, a most wonderful, formidable and sometimes dangerous gift. Hermeneutics enquires into the conditions of understanding that language offers us, the conditions of plausibility. Interpretive humility leads to good and effective dialogue, to the growing insight of an open mind. Our deepest beliefs are mediated through history, tradition and language and we do well to pay attention to the nuances, to the context as well as the text. Marquette theologian D. Stephen Long shows us that we can escape nihilism for something better. He helps us in our ascent towards an integration of faith and reason, towards a personal and social acquisition of the good and goodness. This helps to put our lives and our scholarship into perspective, to show how we can flourish in a more robust, holistic manner, where philosophy and theology join hands.

> Good philosophy, philosophy that does not seek to close us off from the world in some tight, immanent reality, will remain open to receiving this gift, a gift that can be found in language, but never identified with it. Philosophy should be the love of wisdom that prompts persons to use reason in the quest for truth, goodness and beauty.... Philosophy and theology have distinct tasks, but those tasks cannot be delineated solely in terms of nature and supernature or reason and faith. There must be something which is to all beings the cause of their being, goodness, and every other perfection; and this we call God.... Theology comes as gift communicating God's goodness to creatures for their own perfection, showing them their imperfection" (D.S. Long, 2009, 83, 207, 316).

Scholars work with grammar, figures of speech, assumptions, proposals, theories, and arguments encompassing a complex variety of linguistic practice. We ought to explore and enjoy language to the full, for the common good of society, to build up moral capital, to promote *shalom*. To close ourselves off, to implode into a minimalist or reductionist language game, or to try to articulate all aspects of life with scientific language alone, to refuse theological, poetic, artistic and philosophical speech is a move towards a major cultural deprivation and decline. It is to be in denial of this common human heritage, this larger linguistic and moral horizon, the *thick* understanding of human identity. It is to refuse our fullest humanity, to deprive us of the full academic and personal adventure, full flourishing in research, social life and political life.

Finally, on this point of the vertical aspect of language, poet-pastor-theologian Eugene Peterson, a grand wordsmith and astute culture observer of late modernity, speaks to the vital concern with words. He tells us to watch our language, to keep it fresh and vital.

He adds much to the intent of the quote from Professor Long, and helps to capitalize our discussion on the importance of redeeming language. He challenges his fellow Christians to take language more seriously in all of its rich dimensions. It is relevant to all persons who desire to flourish as whole persons.

> Christian followers of Jesus have an urgent mandate to care for language—spoken, heard, written—as a means by which God reveals himself to us, by which we express the truth and allegiance of our lives, and by which we give witness to the Word made flesh .... Contemporary language has been dessicated by the fashions of the academic world (reductive rationalism) and the frenzy of industrial and economic greed (reductive pragmatism). The consequence is that much of the talk in our time has become, well, just talk—not much theological content to it, not much personal relationship involved, no spirit, no Holy Spirit ... We need a feel for vocabulary and syntax that is able to detect and delete disembodied ideas, language that fails to engage personal participation. We need a thorough grounding in the robustness of biblical story and grammar that insists on vital articulated *speech* (not just the employment of words) for the health of the body and mind and soul .... Words don't just sit there, like bumps on a log. They have agency. Scott Cairns, reflecting on his work as a poet working with words in the context of a believing community reading the Scriptures, says that we "are attending not only to a past (an event to which the words refer), but are attending to a present and a presence (which the words articulate into proximity for their apprehension)... leaning into that articulate presence, participating in its energies, and thereby participating in the creation of meaning, with which we help to shape the future" (E. Peterson, 2007, 67-8).

We have made it through the tunnel and out beyond the guards, searchlights and the watchdogs, and we catch wind of a wonderful new world to explore, a whole new adventure that can be ours, if we have the curiosity and courage to pursue it. We hope that you are not yet exhausted, that you can keep the goal in front of you. In the next chapter, we employ the language of *agape* love to inspire us, to turn the lights on to a brave new world, one rife with adventure. We begin mapping the new territory, to find our way to our greatest passion and a stable and just society.

8

Beyond Nihilism

The Transcendent Turn to *Agape* Love

What will give us perspective on our conflicts, help us grapple with our addictions, break down our prejudice, quell the rage and violence inside us? On the other hand, what will help us recover our passion, our creativity, our energy for life? We often want to be more whole, less anxious than we are, but we don't know how to get there. Nietzsche pursued horizontal transcendence by escaping the *all too human* challenges of society on his hikes through the Alps. From that vantage point, he could feel like a god and imagine his superiority and aloofness to normal human struggles. He lived like Zarathustra, the overcomer, high above it all. "Much thought today is a footnote on Nietzsche", observes British social philosopher John Milbank. As a disciple of Nietzsche, Foucault also promoted a horizontal transcendence by means of continuously reinventing the self as a work of art. It was a search for change within the self, much like the story in the movie *Eat, Pray, Love*, a search within the immanent frame, an intra-temporal, self-transcendence. Bored with our circumstances, we often sense the urgency to search for deeper meaning, or to have a make-over. But this *weak* kind of transcendence has its own *glass ceiling*. Many people find themselves on just such a spiritual journey.

Charles Taylor offers something dramatically different in his proposal of a transcendent turn towards *agape* love. It is, according to Taylor, the *strong* type of transcendence, one that does not involve escaping the world. We thank philosopher Calvin Schrag

(1997, 110-148) for his carefully worded insights into the distinction between strong and weak transcendence. In the discussion that follows, we are offering a wager on such strong transcendence as a way to wholeness. George Steiner (*Real Presences*, 1991) is an expert on meaning in the arts. He is very interested in presence and transcendence when it comes to human creations in literature, art, and music. Music, performance, storytelling, painting and poetry offer a conduit to the heart of one's identity and a gateway to the transcendent.

> The arts are most wonderfully rooted in substance in the human body, in stone, in pigment, in twanging of gut or the weight of wind on reeds. All good art and music begin in immanence. But they do not stop there.... It is the enterprise and privilege of the aesthetic to quicken into literal presence, the continuum between temporality and eternity, between matter and spirit, between mankind and 'the other'. It is this common and exact sense that *poiesis* opens onto, is underwritten by the religions and the metaphysical. (G. Steiner, 1991, 227)

Taylor (1989, 490-93) refers to this as the *epiphanic moment*: one quite similar to the *I-Thou* encounter. Many of the great founding moves of a new spiritual direction in history have involved a transformation of the frame (social imaginary) in which people thought, felt and lived. Transcendent encounter brings into view something beyond the frame, while at the same time changing the meaning of all the elements within the frame. Things make sense in a wholly new way. This place of hope offers an expanded horizon of meaning and a fruitful *source* of the moral self. By strengthening agency, it allows us to locate the self in a stance of engagement with the world, not fear of it. It is a courageous move into fuller attentiveness, realization and empowerment. In Chapter 2, we showed the importance of love and embrace, both existentially and relationally. The present discussion extends and expands the concept of love in which we are invested.

We want to explore the transformative impact of the investment, to show how *agape* love in particular opens up space for identity discovery, new self-articulation, and a fresh social vision. Taylor sincerely believes that this understanding of transcendence is critical to one's best and most robust account of the moral world. The refusal to engage a *strong* transcendence is a tragic choice to restrict one's moral imagination, with serious repercussions that people experience daily. Those who reject such vertical transcendence entertain the distinct possibility of imploding back into the *angst* of nihilism, or becoming a victim of the moral chaos of *anomie*.

This *strong* version of transcendence means that, while it comes from outside human culture, it offers transforming dynamics within the economies of the full range of the culture spheres: in science, the arts, ethics and religion. It also brings with it a dimension of depth that may be able to unite these culture spheres. That discussion is another book. Taylor believes that the *epiphanic* discovery of *agape* love can act as a hypergood, in that it influences a rearrangement of one's moral goods, bringing into play both a *transfiguration* and *transvaluation* within the moral self. It offers the fulfilment of our wistful longing, our *sehnsucht*—a critical link between the transcendent (radically other) and the immanent (here and now). Taylor refers to St. Francis, Bede Griffiths, Mother Teresa, G.K. Chesterton, Jacques Maritain, Walker Percy and Gerard Manley Hopkins, as people who benefited greatly from such a wager on strong transcendence. They all discovered a new *social imaginary*, a new way of seeing life. This in turn led to a new kind of flourishing, beyond mere economic security, biological health or longevity of years.

What are the dynamics, the working impact of transcendent *agape* love? It enters the economies of the culture-spheres without being assimilated by any single one of them, breaking open the restrictive hegemony of scientism and deconstructing the ideology of the aesthetic. This strong type of transcendence provides a stance whereby no culture-sphere or ideology can gain full control, or claim a God's-eye viewpoint. Nationalism is currently a rising ideological force that seeks to grab the public imagination in several countries. *Agape* functions as a principle of restraint, for instance, in Foucault's hyper emphasis on the aesthetic, challenging this aesthetic over-interpretation. These ideologies are always contingent and in flux, but they can be virulent and dangerous at the moment of their ascendency, as the history of the twentieth century shows (Paul Johnson, 1983). Ideology often arises out of the soil of relativism. This strong transcendence has the efficacy of a horizon of broad possibilities within those very culture-spheres, protecting them from stifling and trivialization, or other extremes. This is an important note for academia.

How then do these dynamics work? One can experience an *epiphany of transcendence,* which involves an encounter with the radically other, within an episode of realization, revelation and disclosure. Nihilism speaks to absence; transcendence speaks of presence. Michael Morgan, a commentator on Charles Taylor's philosophy, explains how this encounter can change one's entire perspective.

> The self is receiver, but it is a receiver, not of a content, a proposition, a truth, but rather of a 'Presence, a Presence as Power'. Furthermore, that Presence provides 'the inexpressible confirmation of meaning', a meaning that calls out to be done, to be confirmed by the self in this life and in this world ... This confirmation and this affirmation of God and self in the world are what Taylor calls a 'changed stance towards self and world, which doesn't simply recognize a hitherto occluded good, but rather helps to bring this about'. (M. Morgan, 1994, 60)

As the individual encounters the radically transcendent other, he is re-oriented in the presence of the inaccessible or sublime. It involves both an existential encounter and a revelation. This is where one is taken beyond the present realized bounds of one's self to discover new depths. The self is coming in touch with that which lies beyond it, a ground or qualitative pre-eminence. One becomes open to its empowerment. Taylor clarifies using his language of *articulation,* which involves naming a good in its depth, and illuminating its power as an engine for ethical discourse and agency. This is what we mean when we say that God is love.

> The belief in God ... offers a reason ... as an articulation of what is crucial to the shape of the moral world in one's best account. It offers a reason rather as I do when I lay out the most basic concerns in order to make sense of my life to you. (C. Taylor, 1989, 76)

Taylor (1989, 71) does not accept all hypergoods as legitimate, especially those that lead to reductionism, those that abstract the self artificially from the life-world, or distort reality in some way, those that are illusory or a projection of more ignoble interests. But God's love is one active contemporary source of the good, the love of which has empowered people to do the good and exemplify the good in their character, life and politics. This love of such a good is connected to knowledge, giving both beliefs and actions significance. It brings to light or articulates a love transcendent of the human community and culture, but at the same time, it remains accessible to that community. Such *agape* love has made practical sense of life for billions of people down the centuries. It has rearranged their internal priorities.

Taylor believes that transcendent *agape* is a valid hypergood, one that can help us confront and move beyond the anti-humanist, self-destructive forces of late modernity, the *demonic*. He hints at this in *Sources of the Self* (1989) and brings it to full of expression in *A Secular Age* (2007). In its strong transcendence, it can release late moderns from the twin dilemmas of the *crisis of affirmation*: either self-hatred or spiritual lobotomy (C. Taylor, 1989, 495-521). It implies the inability or struggle, in a broken world, to affirm self and the world, to see both the world and the self as good. Either we hate ourselves for moral failure, or we hate the very morality that makes us feel guilty for this failure. Taylor illustrates key consequences of such nihilism through an astute reflection on Dostoyevsky's prophetic novel *The Brothers Karamozov*. He identifies a salient problem to be confronted, one's stance towards grace. It offers some surprising insight into the spirituality of terrorism, and the importance of understanding the difference between good and evil.

> One of Dostoyevsky's central insights turns on the way in which we close or open ourselves to grace. The ultimate sin is to close oneself, but the reasons for doing so can be of the highest. In a sense the person who is closed is in a vicious circle from which it is hard to escape. We are closed to grace, because we close ourselves to the world in which it circulates; and we do that out of loathing for ourselves and for the world .... Rejecting the world seals one's sense of its loathsomeness and of one's own, insofar as one is a part of it. And from this can come only acts of hate and destruction. Dostoyevsky ... gives an acute understanding of how loathing and self-loathing, inspired by the very real evils of the world, fuel a projection of evil outward, a polarization between self and the world, where all evil is now seen to reside. This justifies terror, violence, and destruction against the world; indeed this seems to call for it. No one ... has given us deeper insight into the *spiritual* sources of modern terrorism or has shown more clearly how terrorism can be a response to the threat of self-hatred ... The noblest wreak it [destruction] on themselves. The most base destroy others. Although powered by the noblest sense of the injustice of things, this schism is ultimately also the fruit of pride, Dostoyevsky holds. We separate because we don't want to see ourselves as part of evil; we want to raise ourselves above it. (Taylor, 1989, 451-52)

Taylor offers a thorough overview of how we analyze and wrestle to understand the sources of violence (*A Secular Age,* 2007, 656-710). He suggests that we need a transcendent turn to avoid the extremes of self-hatred, guilt and shame or alternatively the extremity of hating morality itself—*spiritual lobotomy*. The transcendent turn to *agape* becomes vital to solve this problem. Continuing with his discussion concerning Dostoyevsky, Taylor explains how it transforms our perspective and the posture of our being in the world.

> What will transform us is an ability to love the world and ourselves, to see it as good in spite of the wrong. But this will only come to us if we can accept being part of it, and that means accepting responsibility ... Loving the world and ourselves is in a sense a miracle, in face of all the evil and degradation that it and we contain. But the miracle comes on us if we accept being part of it. Involved in this is our acceptance of love from others. We become capable of love through being loved; and over against the perverse apostolic succession [of terror and violence] is a grace-dispensing one. Dostoyevsky brings together here a central idea of the Christian tradition, especially evident in the Gospel of John, that people are transformed through being loved by God, a love that they mediate to one another, on the one hand, with the modern notion of a subject who can help to bring on transfiguration through the stance he takes to himself and the world, on the other ... What he [Dostoyevsky] was opposing was that humans affirm their dignity in separation from the world. (C. Taylor, 1989, 452)

That poses a striking predicament. "The only way to escape fully the draw toward violence", he writes, "lies somewhere in the turn to transcendence—that is, through the full-hearted love of some good beyond life" (Taylor, 1999, 28). This is a most profound insight, one worth pondering and wrestling with for some time. *Agape* love is the *miracle* to address the twin dilemmas of self-hatred and spiritual lobotomy, twin evils of the extreme. The first stance of world rejection is dysfunctional and destructive; the second is courageous, redemptive and realistic. In this *agapic* light, one can affirm both self and the world together. We now define this kind of love in more detail.

What is *Agape* Love?

The hypergood *agape* works itself out in the economy of loving one's neighbor. One might also call it a *force of the soul*. It is a love that finds its ultimate motivation and efficiency in love that is freely given. It is a love that loves for the sake of loving: a non-possessive, disinterested love, a love that loves in spite of being unrequited, a love that expects nothing in return. *Agape* far exceeds the bounds of reciprocity. It cannot be defined in terms of prescriptions for self-realization, radical individualism, enlightened self-interest, or excessive self-reflexivity. It appeals to that which is most noble in humans and senses a draw, a commitment to the needs of other persons. It operates outside the economy of production and consumption, because it is rooted in a higher, deeper, broader *economy of grace*. It includes a willingness to sacrifice self-interest and personal desires, in the interest of community or mutuality.

Gift is an example, where there is no expectation of return, where the receiver must accept the gift without strings attached. Calvin Schrag articulates gift this way (C. Schrag, 1997, 140): "The gift remains radically transcendent to the determination of reciprocity within the economy of goods and services ... the gift displays a surplus of significations that overflow the particulars within the cycle of putative gift exchange." It has a paradoxical nature. But when this *ethos* of grace disappears, manipulation, coercion, contempt and terror often swoop in to take its place. It is delicate and fragile. *Agape* is a strong example of this gift love.

We see the concept articulated in the ancient Hebrew Bible, especially in the Psalms, but also throughout the biblical narrative. Paul, the early Christian apostle-theologian, leverages the concept of *agape* in highly creative ways in his letters to young converts to a new way of seeing life. He reinterprets it, fills the Greek metaphor with fresh meaning that is based in the events of the life, death and resurrection and ascension of Jesus of Nazareth, and its profound impact on the culture of the day. It is at the heart of Paul's insight on the possibilities for greater freedom, identity, stability and personal transformation (I Corinthians 13). These early believers had an epiphany that connected them with something *radically other*. In agreement with the other New Testament authors, especially his fellow apostle John, he continuously announced to them that they are the objects of infinite compassion and that they have entered a new space or lifeworld, with a new identity in Christ community, one that is rife with *agapic* potential.

Increasingly, scholarship is dealing with the important legacy of *agape* and how it has transformed the West from a much more brutal Greco-Roman world, to a more civil society (D. B. Hart, 2009; P. Moser, 2009; T. Jackson, 2015). It is a heritage of human worth, civility and compassion that both non-religious and religious people enjoy. There is protection for the victim and a will to extend rights to everyone, all while reducing human suffering and violence. Taylor feels that this is a hopeful possibility for renewed perspective in a world where people are growing up trapped within the immanent frame, stifled by relativism, and confused by moral solipsism. David Hart (2009) noted that historically, Christians have been known for their concern for the poor, the weak, the uneducated, the marginalized and the unwell. He wishes to correct some popular misconceptions and misinformed history of how Christianity has *destroyed* classical culture. Over the centuries, for instance, Christians have made significant contributions to the culture of the contemporary hospital, including the famous Knights of St. John in the twelfth century.

We suggest that this benevolent humanism emerged because citizens were inspired and empowered by *agape* love. Much creativity and good came of it. Over time, it eventually transformed culture in the ancient world, because it offered an alternative to nihilism. Never perfect or without flaw, Christians discovered this transcendent turn in their identity and it empowered them to be change agents within society, to be counter-cultural within the harsh conditions that surrounded them. *Agape* became a cultural driver toward social change and renewal, as it is to this day. David Hart recalls the following illustrative examples:

> There was ... a long tradition of Christian monastic hospitals for the destitute and the dying, going back to the time of Constantine and stretching from the Syrian and Byzantine East to the Western fringes of Christendom, a tradition that had no real precedent in pagan society. St. Ephraim the Syrian (A.D 306-373), when the city of Edessa was ravaged by plague, established hospitals open to those who were afflicted. St. Basil the Great (A.D. 329-379) founded a hospital in Cappadocia with a ward set aside for the care of lepers, whom he did not disdain to nurse with his own hands. St Benedict of Nursia (A.D. 480-547) opened a free infirmary at Monte Cassino and made care of the sick a paramount duty of the monks .... During the Middle Ages, the Benedictines alone were responsible for more than two thousand hospitals in Western Europe. (D.B. Hart, 2009, 30)

These are empirical and quantifiable outcomes. Indeed, there seems to be much leverage in *agape* to change attitudes, organize people to action, move planeloads of food and medical aid, protect children, provide education, offer a home for refugees, engage disasters and rebuild homes. There is power to stimulate the local economy, heal broken relationships and fight injustice and political oppression. It has made a dramatic difference in attitudes within society, leveraging the world in ways that we can all admire. It has even produced a politics of love (T. Jackson, 2015). This hypergood is one that we are fortunately able to access in late modernity. There are great prospects for reigniting solid hope for constructive personal and social transformation (Jim Wallis, *The (Un)Common Good*, 2014). We will connect with Wallis' vision in Chapter 10.

For the moment, let us explore some of the political implications of *agape*. The world's major faiths do not provide warrant for stark opposition between "moral man" and "immoral society". Nor do they suffer the corrupt idea of the primacy of political or economic power over ethical or moral considerations.

Political institutions must be held accountable in consrructive ways. For Indian intellectual and reformer Mahatma Gandhi, love and self-respect were central to his project of transforming India into a more just society as it gained independence during the mid-twentieth century. He saw an important connection between virtue and power. Inspired by Gandhi's commitment to non-violence, American civil rights leader Dr. Martin Luther King Jr. knew intimately this political language of suffering love. It changed him personally and transformed his social activism, helping him decide on a posture of non-violent *education for equality*. Some scholars see him as the foremost American public intellectual of the late twentieth century. He has inspired millions with the possibilities for *agape*. "Love was the supreme unifying principle of his life", writes Dr. Timothy Jackson (*Political Agape*, 2015, 381-408) in a splendid articulation of how this played out in his extraordinary public influence. He knew *agape* as the prophetic stance against white rage, the miracle to bring equality and mutual respect between races and people groups, necessary to heal some of the dark narrative of slavery and racism in America. The movement began with Rosa Parks revealing her dignity on a bus.

William Greenway captures Taylor's trajectory along this profound and fruitful line of reasoning. It resonates with King's philosophy of social change.

> Taylor hopes for a participation with the divine that returns us to this world in such a way that we are able fully to embrace our deepest spiritual aspirations and fully to affirm the world, others, and ourselves without spiritual mutilation and without simply denying the reality of suffering and evil—a miraculous transformation indeed ... As a thinker situated within the mainstream of Western culture ... Taylor's proposed path to resolution of the crisis of affirmation involves appeals to God, grace, and agape, and there is no *a priori* reason to judge these appeals false or misleading. (W. Greenway, 2000, 38-9)

It is worth delving into this fascinating concept in more detail, to see just how it might assist late moderns in their struggle with identity, in their journey from nihilism to substantial meaning, and consequentially deep joy.

By stark contrast, a CBC exclusive news documentary on North Korean prison camps suggests that there are places in the world today where *agape* love is noticeably absent. In North Korea, humans are treated with contempt, worse than animals at times, society is not functioning properly, the élites do not operate on servant leadership principles. Cruelty by prison guards in the multiple camps throughout the country reaches new dark depths. The government of dictator Kim Jong-un is one of the most secretive and oppressive regimes in the world and a pending nuclear threat. Political debate is not tolerated and opponents to the regime are summarily eliminated as in the case of many generals, including his own uncle. Lies and propaganda rule while life is often fearful, miserable, brutal and short. Human rights are not respected. In this living anti-humanist dystopia, the nihilistic absence of love matters. It is replaced by coercion, contempt, violence and terror. On a similar note, Rosemary Sullivan (2015) has captured the tortured and tragic life of Stalin's daughter, Svetlana Alliluyeva, who grew up around such brutality: where friends and family members were eliminated out of political paranoia or mere dislike, where writers and artists were imprisoned in huge numbers in the Gulag. It was shocking to eventually discover just how oppressive was the father that she had loved as a girl. Imagine living in such a shadow. Many people around the world want to move to the West where there is a stronger emphasis on human dignity, rights and one's personal voice, a heritage of *agape* love.

Cognitive Barrier to Agape

But today's cynic might test our proposal and ask why we do not see more evidence of such love in the world. This is a complex puzzle, one that is worth trying to resolve. Some of us may even have trouble reading and discerning this language of *agape*. It is often caricatured as a weakness, as it was by Nietzsche: pathetic sentimentality or pity. The cynic reads the New Testament story with blurred vision, blind to the possibilities discussed in that great, life-giving narrative of heaven interfacing with earth. Many late moderns have problems believing in such a love, such spiritual food. It is not part of their daily conversation. Skeptics often want to treat evidence of *agape* love, and evidence for God, like a laboratory investigation. They cannot see the sign in the Advent, cannot discern the import of the storyline of the woman at the well who was seeking living water in order to become whole. They cannot fully grasp the profundity and reform value of the liberating Sermon on the Mount, nor can they understand the reasoning behind the Good Samaritan story. It is a story that depicts compassion for a stranger or outsider, even an enemy. They are baffled and bemused by scholars who would travel the globe to investigate, to do deep archaeological research or spend their whole career investigating the backstory of *agape* love. There is no feeling of wonder at the Advent miracle or the earthshaking consequences of the resurrection of the Christ. Handicapped by moral blockage, blinded by scientism, cynics do not acknowledge divine love *prima facie*. We suggest that it is a phenomenon we can call a *spiritual cataract*.

Solve this puzzle we must. Is such a love too fanciful, too distant from our experience of reality, sullied as we are with jealousy and gossip, relational brokenness, greed and egotism, terror and violence, hatred and racism? Are we settling for absence and emptiness, all the while missing the miracle of divine presence and fullness, the deepest longings of our hearts? Are many of us looking for God in all the wrong places, using the wrong filters? Do we proclaim that he and his love are irrelevant to our highest aspirations? Do we have the wrong research methodology, or outdated interpretive tools? Is there a controlling intellectual bias (a *blik*) blocking our view? Has dogmatic rationalism shut out the transcendent that still haunts us, even in our 'secular age'? If God is in love with human beings, obsessed with their wellbeing, why is it not more evident? Let us examine the nuances.

Hermeneutics of Humility

Loyola University philosopher Paul Moser offers guidance and insight on this problem. He suggests that we often misunderstand the rules of engagement. As a counterpoint to the skeptic's dismissal of the evidence, dismay and mental block, Dr. Moser reframes the investigation: "Are we humans in a position on our own to answer the question of whether God exists, without our being morally challenged by God?" (P.K. Moser, 2009, 49-64). Revelation of this sort involves an encounter, divine cognitive grace engaging stony, resistant hearts and skeptical minds. This is what we have been hinting at throughout this dialogue. Nihilism is not our liberator but our jailer. It owns our minds and hearts as captives.

We ask, "What kind of person will actually discover God, feel divine presence, experience and be transformed by the holy communion of *agape*?" Courage, patience and perseverance may help keep the investigation open. Yes of course, there is no magic cognitive bullet to answer all of our questions, especially the ones about tragedy, evil and suffering, and the death of innocents. But there may be an alternative posture available, one that can lead to different results. There may be hope of knowing and experiencing the transcendent God as love. If we are stuck in our reasoning, it might help us to find some new interlocutors, people who offer a different outlook, and a listening ear.

Evidence for the God of *agape* love is not a scientific process, where we treat him as a laboratory animal. Many of us have had this type of late night impish discussion in dorms or at the local pub. Rather, says Moser circumspectly, it requires the seeker to approach with humility and undergo a personal examination. We need a new interpretive grid (David Brooks, 2015; Paul Moser, 2009). Pride blocks the road to insight into this all-important big question. Moser informs us that we need the right *motivation of the heart* to deal properly with the *hidden* God. We need healing from our cynicism in order to see and perceive, discern and decipher.

So when exactly do the data and questions prove revelatory and plausible? Let us try a thought experiment. What if the fundamentals in life are not cosmos, nebulae and galaxies, matter and energy, time, space, forces and motion, protons and electrons, quarks and gluons? What if instead they are love, joy, peace and goodness, I-Thou relationship, purity of the inner self? What if taking responsibility for our neighbor, loving our enemy, is one of the most fundamental and important principles of life, even more fundamental that the law of gravity itself? Is love the core explanation of reality, the deepest depth? Again, brilliant Marquette University professor D. Stephen Long captures this insight:

> Only on the basis of an ontology of love can gift be understood. Because love, and not pure reason, is the basic structure of being, the failure of human reason to achieve infinite desires is not negative but positive. Thus we do not need to negate reason in order to believe, but rather to supplement and intensify it. We receive knowledge as a gift. ... Gift, another name for the Holy Spirit, is the fullness of being, the perfection that surrounds us with an inevitable desire for truth, goodness and beauty. It illumines our lives. For Wittgenstein, truth is not a matter of detachment, but engagement, the kind of engagement that love entails and that requires judgments based on qualitative contrasts.... Wittgenstein's appeal to love depends on something more akin to 'virtue epistemology'. Love is not opposed to truth; they are both necessary virtues for knowledge. You cannot know what you do not love; you cannot love what you do not know. (D.S. Long, 2009, 159, 300-1)

This investigation is not just about the first cause, or the evidence of a designer in a fine-tuned universe, as interesting and evocative as that may be. *Agape* itself sets the parameters for discovery and the rules of engagement. This provocative quote offers a breakthrough in the faith-reason discussion, a major plank in a platform for fruitful reflection and dialogue. What if gratitude and humility are the hermeneutical key that we skeptics are searching for, at the very core of reality (as opposed to raw power or matter)? What if transitory material things are *signs* or expressions of God's love?

Agape love is, we suggest, a cultural and spiritual Holy Grail, a win-win discovery for atheists, agnostics, seekers and nihilists as well as believers, people from various religious backgrounds. God may indeed show up for those who stop their cynical rant and attend more carefully to his positive, sometimes subtle, gestures and initiatives. The spirit and posture with which we attend to the details makes all the difference. At that point, the investigation goes through a radical recalibration. The data that was previously ignored or discarded can now be re-examined for its pertinence, immediacy and relevance. A paradigm shift will occur over time, as the data of our experience is reassessed. God's *agape* love directed at the human conscience is actually a deep invitational call to an existential depth. Late moderns from around the globe are capable of experiencing disclosure of the *gift* in the midst of transformation. *Agape* offers an enlightening grace that shines a scintillating light on inner depths and motivations.

According to this outlook, Foucault's focus on *beauty or the art of self* is revealed as an *agape* substitute. There are many others. Moser poses the critical question: "Are we sincerely attending to the divine call via conscience and experienced *agape* in a way that leads us before the God of Abraham, Isaac, Jacob and Jesus?" (P. Moser, 2009, 61) Humility is a key posture or virtue in this quest. David Brooks agrees with this posture of humility in regards to moral growth (D. Brooks, *The Road to Character*, 2015, 261-7).

This produces a refraction of light from lived experience through a different prism to produce new insights and vision. A new picture of reality begins to form and come into focus. Within the horizon of *agape,* there is a move from shame to self-respect, vengeance to forgiveness, alienation for outsiders to support and protection for victims. There is an offer of reconciliation with one's deepest and most fragmented self, compassion for the poor, even concern for one's enemies.

A New Humanism

Such a heritage is worthy of recovery. More will be said about the humanist conversation in Chapter 10, but here are a few preliminary thoughts from religion and culture scholar Jens Zimmermann.

> Understanding the nature of reason is central to our conception of human existence. We have to resist a narrow conception of human rationality that excludes religion as irrational because such a view cripples our ability to analyze correctly the current state of Western culture. As Rodney Stark has argued in his book *The Victory of Reason*, Christianity's ability to combine faith and reason with a progressive view of human nature laid the foundation for Western science and technological progress.... Building on Judaism, Christianity also allowed for the concepts of human dignity, personhood and individuality that have decisively shaped Western views of society.... Neither the best nor the worst features of modernity are comprehensible without the transformative influence of Christianity on Greco-Roman culture. Without religion, the West would not be what it is, and without understanding the religious roots of Western culture and their continuing influence on Western thought, we lack the self-understanding necessary to address our current cultural crisis (J. Zimmermann, 2012a, 25 & 26).

Charles Taylor adds weight to this comment, showing how the agape principle breaks one out of the circle of despair and moral self-mutilation. One can engage suffering and evil, victimization and deception, from the vantage point of such a horizon. This is all part of a positive, constructive, and renewed anthropology. It is one rooted in servanthood and good stewardship (see also J. Richard Middleton, 2005).

> Our being in the image of God is also our standing among others in the stream of love, which is that facet of God's life we try to grasp, very inadequately, in speaking of the Trinity. Now it makes a whole lot of difference whether you think this kind of love is a possibility for us humans. I think it is, but only to the extent that we open ourselves up to God, which means in fact, overstepping the limits set by Nietzsche and Foucault. (C. Taylor, 1999, 35)

This speaks to the ground of *one-anotherness,* creating space for others. It is ironic for Taylor to suggest that Foucault, the *philosopher of freedom,* the one who transgresses limits, sets down a glass ceiling and walls that stifle important potential for self-constitution. It also deprives us of some very significant sources of the self that can empower us morally, artistically, intellectually, and existentially.

Agape is a more precious resource than we dare imagine. It remains that personal and cultural resource that late moderns need to renew society and bring justice to fruition. Taylor pushes us forward on the creativity and vitality of such rich language.

> The original Christian notion of *agape* love is of a love that God has for humans, which is connected with their goodness as creatures (though we don't have to decide whether they are loved because good or good because loved). Human beings participate through grace in this love. There is a divine affirmation of the creature, which is captured in the repeated phrase in Genesis 1 about each stage of the creation, "and God saw that it was good". Agape is inseparable from such "seeing-good". (C. Taylor, 1989, 516)

This 'seeing-good' of others, who are both similar and different than us, renders implausible such stances as prejudice, exclusion, hatred, racism, terrorism, and chauvinism. The individual self is elevated and enhanced by this love, affirmed in dignity and destiny, set free to love, to show hospitality, build community and care for the marginalized. To open ourselves to be loved by God is a profound experience that transforms us and shapes our identity. It can reach the deepest depths. If one sees and feels her worth in God's eyes after a divorce, one may gain the courage to begin to trust again from a position of confidence in her own worthiness (Brené Brown, 2012).

Agape love informs and offers definition and content to the qualities of the will, to one's important choices. Transcendent goodness empowers, clarifies, and animates the human soul. It acknowledges the value that each person gains from the recognition, mercy and affirmation of God—his generous embrace. It is like the light from a thousand suns. Given this *ethos*, the individual does not struggle to define himself and invent a unique universe, but rather discovers some greater context for his identity. Humanity is called forward on a journey to spiral upward together towards mountaintop heights. This is a plausible thought experiment that we will continue to examine in more detail in Chapter 10.

A New Outlook

It is the explanatory adequacy of materialistic naturalistic that we call into question, as do philosophers like Thomas Nagel (2012), Alvin Plantinga (2012) and David Bentley Hart (2013). Our experience of morality and consciousness asks for more.

> Living in a post-secular world means that secularism is no longer the standard for reasonable thought. If indeed it is true that Western culture continues to experience a crisis of identity and purpose, the dogmatic exclusion of sources of transcendent purpose (i.e. religion) seems unwise.... Such dogmatism is not secular thinking, if *secular* is taken at its root meaning of "this worldly". Rather, the arbitrary exclusion of religion from reasonable discourse is *secularist ideology,* a fundamentalist rejection of all interpretation of the world, except the materialist one that excludes religion. (J. Zimmermann, 2012a, 41)

Christians claim that a progressive anthropology towards a *thick* self involves *agape*. It can be seen most clearly in the God-man Jesus Christ. We will explore this important topic in Chapter 10. This is the "exit" that Danish philosopher Søren Kierkegaard wrote about, an exit from the burden of a self-reflexive loop of despair. It is hard to cope when the entire burden of creating meaning is on our shoulders, up to our individual creativity. It can become a confining world, where we are trapped by the smallness of our own self-interest and desires. We long to break free of it.

We need a fresh meta-biology perspective. On this note, it may be helpful to tell the story of Daniel, a student in his early days as an undergraduate at Queen's University. Coming in as a country mouse to the city of Kingston, he felt quite vulnerable as he discovered a whole new world, one with multifaceted viewpoints on everything he held sacred. He quickly realized that every belief he had ever countenanced was to be contested. In search of new friends and community, he was quite overwhelmed amidst a sea of faces and conflicting opinions and worldviews on campus. At first, Daniel only found friendship in bits and pieces here and there. The sense of belonging that community usually provides was frustratingly elusive. Unfortunately, loyalties can be short-lived in a utilitarian world where fellow students all attempt to climb the ladder of success, and seek the few openings available in medicine, law or graduate school. Eventually by third year, Daniel discovered support in its fullness in a Christian community near campus where *agape* love was palpable, abundant and consistent.

This community was known for its hospitable stance towards students. They were included and even celebrated like extended family. Daniel was embraced and inspired, experiencing a new fullness and wholeness in his student experience. He had found a community of soulmates, students and families with whom to grow morally, spiritually and personally. In this context, he gained the confidence to engage the tough questions about his faith on campus. These sincere young men and women learned to think together, while pushing out their intellectual boundaries and grappling with global issues. In this environment of lived *agape* and careful biblical teaching, he flourished in his faith and enjoyed so many fruitful friendships, many of whom tracked with him for his entire life. This epiphany of *agape* love gave Daniel new hope and vision for the world. Moreover, it opened up his life goals to new horizons, giving birth to a powerful dream of a better world. As they graduated, Daniel and his peers felt empowered to make a difference in this wonderful and broken world. They left the all-too-common cynicism behind.

Daniel's fourth year Life Science class of twenty-three students also began to take the shape of an academic community. Weathered by the battles of intense student life, they began to take each other more seriously and cherish each other with the respect of fellow warriors. It was a four year storm of learning and wrestling with competence, identity, career and purpose. They became more of a community than just an assorted array of students, becoming more open with each other about their identities, uncertainties and aspirations for the future. "What's next?" they would often ask each other. They were still competitors for graduate school and medicine, but now realized a stronger sense of collegiality and mutual respect. Thus, questions of meaning and spiritual longing often arose among them. It was an intense but beautiful experience as they saw the end of a major chapter in their lives. Several individuals in that very bright, ambitious class were open to discussing this *agape* love that had gripped Daniel's imagination and changed his outlook. They were curious, even though transcendence to them seemed strange, almost surreal. For many, it was a question of whether they could believe in love itself. Daniel was fully convinced by now that it could be real and life-giving, adding good texture to their aspirations and expectations of life. They should expect more. Both these experiences of community came to be treasured by Daniel as a genuine, unexpected *gift*. A more recent account of the campus search for meaning can be found in the beautiful story *Surprised by Oxford* by Carolyn Weber (2013). As a side note, there are now about one thousand students in Life Sciences at Queen's all hoping to become a doctor.

This story illustrates something salient about life. It is the same gift, the same breakthrough insight into the human condition that is needed in today's political theatre, both in the first world and developing nations, Global South and North. Former Canadian Senator and Peacekeeper Roméo Dallaire (*Shake Hands with the Devil*, 2003) underlined the issue of love in a speech in Vancouver, Canada in May of 2014. He witnessed firsthand the Rwandan genocide and was completely ill-equipped to stop the mayhem. He saw the event as a testimony to what the loss of love and humanism, the literal failure of humanity, can do to devastate a people. He witnessed how human beings can fall so far below their potential, so as to embody evil and carry out a monstrous, organized brutality and murder innocent people. These good people in Rwanda were capable of sinking to frightening, dark depths, and we are too. This terrible experience has inspired him to set up an agency dedicated to rescue child soldiers. Tragically, many children were used to murder 800,000 innocents systematically in Rwanda in this paranoid bloodbath. *Agape* was subverted by unbelievable violence organized by militia thugs, as spiritual darkness fell over the land. The healing of the nation could only come through a recovery of transcendent goodness and *agape* love: forgiveness, reconciliation, and a gradual new hope of loving and trusting one's neighbor again. It takes time and much grace, as a Rwandan Ph.D. student in Oxford explained to us. It is parallel to the situation in South Africa where Desmond Tutu led the *Truth and Reconciliation Commission*. He along with Nelson Mandela and many other noble souls went up against racism, potential social chaos and dark memories of oppression with hearts full of tough love, offering a profound impact towards healing a broken nation. This is the power of the *politics of agape*.

Now we must ask ourselves, can *agape* anchor our lives, sort out the crisis of identity in late modernity, and show us the way home spiritually, the way to the heart of meaning? Could it be the miracle for which we have secretly been longing? Charles Taylor in the chapter called "Conversions" (C. Taylor, 2007, 728-772) reviews several examples of individuals who have been transformed by a transcendent turn to *agape* love from within the immanent frame: Gerard Manley Hopkins, Charles de Foucauld, John Maine, Jean Vanier, Mother Teresa, and Thérèse de Lisieux. Each has a unique and life changing spiritual journey.

Academia and the Potential of a Virtuous Community

We now want to see if we can leverage this concept of *agape* within the university setting, to explore the question of whether love can make a difference in collegiality. As Charles Taylor often said, "High standards require strong sources." Our universities set some of the highest standards intellectually. But many who enter the academy have high expectations of character excellence as well. Sometimes, however, they are shocked with the lack of it in some fellow participants. What kind of person forms, or is drawn to, a virtuous community? Is it possible for a university to become such a community, or at least move in the direction of a humanism inspired by love? In the long history of the university, character formation was a central priority for education. But can we find traces of this trajectory in the now and future university?

We are certainly familiar with the vices of people in our department, the willingness of others to exploit our vulnerabilities, steal our resources, take credit for our work, familiar with other universities head hunting our best scholars. We know the pressures to perform in a highly competitive environment. The vices are alive and well. But John Sommerville (2006) is one of several scholars who mourn the crisis of the modern university. He sees it as a crisis of values that have been lost from the long heritage of higher education. Education is essential for self-awareness and a key source for sustaining the conditions for democracy and civil society, as well as the economy. At the same time, education is under intense pressure from various forces, both intrinsic and extrinsic. These forces are currently pulling it in different directions, amidst conflicting public expectations. Will the old idea of a liberal arts education survive into the middle twenty-first century in our hyper-competitive skills-based economy?

How then do we locate ourselves with respect to the good? What do wisdom, courage and hope, benevolence and compassion have to do with scholarship? What do virtues like moderation, self-restraint and frugality, patience and gratitude have to do with academic excellence, business acumen or scientific and technological skills? Does higher education encourage the pursuit of both academic excellence and character development of students in any sustainable way? We know universities have to be highly innovative and socially relevant in order attract students from home and abroad. Yet a question lingers. Do they prepare students for negotiating an increasingly complex and competitive globalized world? What will inspire and engage their imagination in the pursuit of citizenship and civil discourse, or their understanding of other cultures? What will fire their imagination in the pursuit of truth from all corners? Can virtue inform our academic vision which in turn shapes our goals and actions, especially our relationship with colleagues? Are virtuous people suckers for those who would willingly exploit them or are they the cutting-edge servant leaders of tomorrow that add new value to culture, and offer the skills that we need for a better world economy?

Many know of the highly influential work of philosopher Alasdair MacIntyre (*After Virtue,* 2007). He attempts to remedy the cultural loss of this ancient language of virtue, in a similar way to Taylor's (1989) attempt at recovery of the good for moral discourse. In its place, many late moderns have substituted Max Weber's language of values, an aesthetic, Nietzschean concept. MacIntyre is broadly influential in challenging academia to remember its heritage in virtue ethics. Indeed, virtue ethics has recently made a strong comeback as an area of study. One UBC philosophy professor, Paul Russell, was given a grant of twenty million dollars by the Swedish government to research ethics, human freedom, choice and virtue. This is notable. After all, both personal and intellectual virtue is terribly relevant to today's academic world and to society at large.

Virtue is a *strong* characteristic of a person or an institution. Leisure intellectual Joseph Pieper (1954) wrote a classic called *The Four Cardinal Virtues.* A moral virtue can be described as an excellence of character, developed by conscious choices over time. For this, the individual or institution should be praised. Virtue is a good cultivated and practiced habit. It disposes one to act in a reasonable way and to avoid extreme positions, to act in short as a sage would act, applying discernment or *phronesis.* Virtues are heuristic in that they teach us about new dimensions, delicate nuances to life as we embrace them and embody them. They take us deeper and reveal to us what kind of character we trust in others and why. Once we enter the discourse and the practice of virtue, its implications are impressive and extensive. Virtues have a direct connection to justice, as both Plato and Aristotle understood. Justice always involves a certain turning around and transformation of self-centered dispositions, a certain kind of faithfulness to others and to principled living. It involves movement to higher moral ground. Justice and virtue are ends in themselves, not just a means to other ends like power or wealth.

What a privilege to be mentored in the virtues. Many have appreciated such influences. These include parents, teachers, coaches, business and government leaders, and university faculty members who inspire a noble life, going the extra mile, involving personal sacrifice and goodness. Recently deceased Dr. Philip Hill, a professor from Mechanical Engineering at University of British Columbia, was this kind of exceptionally generous exemplar for many students and fellow faculty. Known for the virtue of hospitality alongside a deep commitment to his craft, he and his family had a huge impact for the good within the academic community. Dr. Hill had the ability to give intense attention to individual students and to draw out their strengths. Another significant mentor in the virtues is environmental theologian Steven Bouma-Prediger (*For the Beauty of the Earth, 2010*), from Hope College, Michigan. He shared his concern for environmental stewardship virtues as a visiting scholar at UBC. At a young age, he enjoyed hiking in various parts of the world and eventually developed a vision for building a project to preserve this beauty for posterity, for his children and grandchildren. In his writing, he displays an exceptional gift and sensibility of wordcraft, both philosophically and theologically, as he exposits the language of virtues and vices regarding human consumption and our relationship to the biosphere. He is a person of both theoretical and practical vision. His idea is that we have to see the biosphere as our *home* and offer the same care that we would to our own sacred living space. Here's how he defines virtue.

> A virtue is a state of praiseworthy character—with the attendant desires, attitudes and emotions. Formed by choices over time, a virtue disposes us to act in certain excellent ways. Knowing which way is the truly excellent way involves avoiding the extremes of vice by looking to people of virtue as role models. As certain virtues shape our character, they influence how we see the world. And the entire process of forming virtues is shaped by a particular narrative and community. The settled disposition to act well, which makes us who we are, is nurtured by the stories we imbibe and the communities of which we are a part. (S. Bouma-Prediger, 2010, 140)

Bouma-Prediger applies the discourse powerfully to a philosophy of environmental stewardship, which he sees as a communal effort. There is an art or finesse, a personal strength and creativity to virtue in the *strong* sense. Virtues orient us in moral space, towards both individual and group flourishing, and also flourishing of our bio-physical home. It takes the whole picture into account regarding responsible action and attitudes. It is ecological in flavor, involving integral rather than narrow or one-sided thinking. Virtues are good for society, promoting trustworthy relationships that are characteristic of a moral community. It takes into consideration the individual as well as the common good. Quentin Schultze (2002, 165-88) writes about nurturing virtue in community as he relates to the high tech subculture. For him, virtue pursues communion and a sense of *place,* not merely communication in a *placeless* world: "Dialogue is an act of making ourselves available for community" (Q. Schultze, 2002, 187). Thus, the idea of a community of virtue is not so far-fetched.

There are also academic or research virtues, such as thoroughness, perseverance to follow the evidence, intellectual honesty, conscientiousness in pursuit of truth, fair treatment of students, as shown by Linda Zagzebski (*Virtues of the Mind,* 1996). These virtues help the university keep its integrity of scholarship as a holistic and credible knowledge center. Love is also a key component of the search for truth. Oxford University's deceased Iris Murdoch (1997) had a high view of the transcendent moral good, and she inspired Charles Taylor in this vision as a DPhil student at All Souls College. She knew the cash-out value of virtue, and valued the concept of a good person, and respected the power of being inspired by the good. It was not adequate that these ideals, transcendentals like truth, beauty and goodness, be simply replaced by human desires. Murdoch bears some of the responsibility for Taylor's monumental contribution to the recovery of the ancient language of the good, and for his immense contribution in our understanding of late modernity. What an intellectual treasure trove her mentorship has bequeathed us. People who have a vision for mentoring future leaders see the importance of virtue, and enjoy witnessing the growth in character in their novices. As we see in the struggles of various significant persons in David Brooks fine work, *The Road to Character* (2015), the virtues and vices of a public leader have a vast cultural impact.

Early Modern European historian, Brad Gregory (2012, 180-233) from Notre Dame University, also contributes strongly to any discussion on virtue in his brilliant tome *The Unintended Reformation* We refer in particular to the chapter called *Subjectivizing Morality*. He traces pertinent changes in cultural and moral language and landscape over five hundred years, the same period covered by Charles Taylor's tome *A Secular Age*. He draws to our attention a time when the virtuous community was a common social and political consciousness in Europe, part of people's normal corporate identity. Virtue had a much larger currency at one time. Much of this has been lost in recent years, amidst globalization and the increasing plurality of cultural convictions—James Davison Hunter calls this phenomenon *difference*. Gregory's claim is that virtue has been exchanged for a utilitarian, self-focused language of rights, a much more nihilistic stance. This is quite a reversal of outlook from the original idea of rights as we might find in Jacques Maritain.

> A transformation from a substantive morality of the good to a formal morality of rights constitutes the central change in Western ethics over the past half millennium, in terms of theory, practice, laws and institutions. Moreover, there is a historical relationship between the creation of ethics of rights and the antecedent ethics of the good that it displaced, a shift that involves much more than the institutionalized triumph of putatively superior ethical and political ideas.... Once the metaphysical basis of an ethics of the good has been jettisoned, nothing remains in principle but the human will and its desires protected by the state.... An ethics of rights displaced and marginalized a substantive Christian ethics of the good even as it continued to draw on it, and thus fostered the subjectivization of morality. (B. Gregory, 2012, 184 and 189)

This insightful statement offers a profound look into how the language of the good and virtue was lost from the discourse of moral philosophy, buried deeply. At one time, rights were articulated within the values framework of the communal good, within the discourse of the virtuous community. Now, rights have morphed into a vulgar commodity: where it is paramount to fulfill *my* individual subjective desires, opinions, entitlements or consumer choices (an unchecked wish list of conflicting subjective wants). Our individual desires and interests seem to be in tension, even conflict, with the common good, within a discourse of radical individualism. It involves the veneration of choice and entails the intoxicating promise of limitless freedom. As a result, we are struggling to find the social glue or common purpose to hold society together and to give it a fecund trajectory. We struggle and suffer with the loss of a moral center that can keep us from fragmenting into factions. Perhaps it can be at least partially recovered with some effort by the conversation in this book and the dialogue and debate that ensues.

Can we recover and leverage the power of virtue and the power of *agape*, that supreme virtue of *caritas,* for the university, church and society, and for all four culture spheres? The Apostle Paul believed that *agape* was the hub (I Corinthians 13), the supervirtue from which all other virtues radiated, and that the imitation of Christ's sacrificial love provided the standard for living a certain kind of life, a life of gratitude, abundance and joy. The recovery of the language of virtue is a move towards a significant attentiveness and engagement with reality. We believe that it is not only possible, but necessary, for our flourishing within a civil society and a healthy scholarly and sustainable university community. Recovery of virtue is a very urgent concern.

Some wise seniors and retired professors can pass on these virtues of character to the emerging generation of young scholars (James Houston, *The Mentored Life: From Individualism to Personhood,* 2012). Some mindful university faculty members across North America have been meeting in small groups or gathering around scholarly lectures and seminars on campuses to discuss their heartfelt values and to encourage one another in the virtues (*Transforming Conversations: a guide to mentoring communities among colleagues in higher education* written by Peter Felten, H. Dirksen L.

Bauman, Aaron Kheriaty and Edward Taylor, 2013). These communities provide a valuable source of encouragement and natural accountability around the higher virtues of life, research and teaching. Discussion centers such as the Veritas Forums, Pascal Lectures at University of Waterloo, the Gifford Lectures in Edinburgh, The Faraday Institute for Science and Religion at Cambridge University, and the Ian Ramsey Center for Science and Religion at Oxford University are other great examples of highlighting virtues and grappling with the big questions within the academy. They have all been keen to promote the compatibility between faith and reason, virtue and scholarship. But virtue also needs to penetrate the politics of faculty associations, administrations and the Board of Governors. Contemplation is needed alongside investigation, publication lists and academic prizes.

Next we transition to the articulation of this divine-human interface of the good and *agape* love by way of a discussion on the Holy Spirit, the divine source of moral motivations, and the most direct connection to the divine communion of love. This will take our journey one step further and improve our map of the journey. It is a key part of this transcendent turn: with a view to enhance human flourishing and make the link to the social *praxis* of love.

9

Beyond Nihilism

Resolving the Problem of Moral Motivation

We have awoken from our nihilist slumber, escaped through the tunnel, and found ourselves in a new world, beyond the barbed wire and the barking dogs and out of range of the sniper's rifle. Now we must learn how to cope and manoeuver in this new environment, to negotiate the opportunities. There is still work to do, more problems to solve, on the journey beyond nihilism. Yale Professor of Ethics John E. Hare (1996) points out an important problem for ethics, which he calls the *moral gap*. One could also refer to it as the problem of moral motivation, as in Charles Taylor's concept of the constitutive good. Let us unpack the issues.

Virtue or one's relationship with the good can place a heavy burden on the individual, a demand for sacrifice. This demand can seem to be in tension with an individual's personal happiness (self-interest), something that Immanuel Kant recognized. If one takes responsibility for the wellbeing of others or the common good, it often requires *sacrifice* of self-interest, personal goals or desires, in order to help others towards their wellbeing. Good examples include raising children, or caring for elderly parents, or an ailing spouse with Alzheimer's disease, or helping with the homeless. The good of my interests comes in conflict with the flourishing of the other. What motivates us to do such a thing? Will we be motivated to do the right think, even when it is the difficult or challenging thing?

This creates a serious problem for both moral motivation and justification. It is an unresolved problem for many moral philosophers, especially Utilitarians, who want to maximize happiness. Why should we make the sacrifices that we know we ought? Let us be honest, we all ask that question at some point. Dr. Hare notes that this is precisely where religion can play a key role as a vital factor in solving the moral gap dilemma. In order to reconcile care for morality (justice) and care for oneself (personal peace and happiness), we need an outside (transcendent) motivator to resolve the tension. Otherwise, how can such justice and peace embrace? How can I love my neighbor and love myself as well? At this juncture, we begin to explore how God helps motivate the individual to meaningful sacrifice of self-interest (a kind of suffering) in order to build the moral space for the common good, to build community and take responsibility for others, to "make more room for more being" as Andy Crouch signaled.

It becomes clear that humans need something more than just moral ideals or knowledge of moral goods in order to meet the moral demand. Otherwise, they could be riddled with guilt and self-hatred, or resentment due to failure. The biblical principle of *shalom,* the concept of blessing, offers the reconciliation between the moral demand (aspirations to the good) and personal meaning. The grace factor is important once again. We perceive the need for an interface between the human moral theatre and the divine in order to resolve this dilemma. Otherwise, we can feel stuck or frustrated. What is the human possibility for *animus,* or motivation for mediating a hypergood that is transcendent of self, one that has purchase on us?

Taylor's transcendent turn to *agape* love lights the journey forward. He suggests that there is a boon in considering *agape* love (*caritas* or God-sourced love) as a *constitutive* (motivational) good within this philosophical turn, in order to animate ethical agency once again. He extends the thought further in his most recent book *A Secular Age* (2007, 756): "A new poetic language can serve to find a way back to the God of Abraham." Abraham was both blessed, and called to bless the other nations, to love his neighbors. *Agape* love is such a poetic-expressive, world-making language. We find this in the works of both Gerard Manley Hopkins and T.S. Eliot as poets who recover language from its flatness. We want to demonstrate in this chapter how the Holy Spirit answers this concern, and brings back the poetry of ethical life.

Recently, we had a telling conversation with a single Swiss woman in her early forties about her conversion from nihilism to faith. She mentioned that in her spiritual journey, she started out believing in God as a child, but her education eventually wiped these beliefs and concerns from her meaning horizon. Education essentially discredited God in her mind. She put the *thoughts of childhood* behind her and bought into a Nietzschean worldview and became an atheist. Unlike Americans, the Swiss do not freely talk about God in public spaces, so it was a long way back. She lost the transcendent dimension of life entirely and entered a nihilist slumber for several years, not realizing that she had become a prisoner of an ideology. All was fine for a while, but one night in her adult life, she had a dream that was like an earthquake to her sense of reality, an encounter with some dark and frightening entity. As a result, she could no longer believe in the absence of the spiritual realm, or the loss of distinction between good and evil. This dark encounter was with something insidious. What entailed was a long search, but eventually, she recovered an adult, mature faith in God, which also recovered *agape* love. If evil was real, there must be a source of good as well, she thought. She had finally awoken, as if from a coma, and shared with us how important the Holy Spirit was as a source in this process. We told her how deeply relevant her story was to the theme of this book and this particular problem of moral motivation.

With this in mind, it is crucial knowledge that the Holy Spirit, as a member of the Trinity, is a key mediator, inspiration and transformation force in human goodness. The presence of God through the Spirit impacts human motivation, justification, and discovery of divine goodness. Marquette theologian D. Stephen Long (2001) is optimistic about the human quest for the good for this reason. It is not futile or merely theoretical, because humans are not left to their own devices in order to build a relationship with the good, nor do they have to come up with motivation for the embrace of a good such as *agape*. Long believes that through the Holy Spirit, moral self-constitution can be intimately and fruitfully related to the infinite goodness of God.

> The Holy Spirit *infuses* a goodness into us that makes us better than we know we are by ourselves. This *better* is what theologians mean by *grace*. People find themselves caught up in a journey that results in the cultivation of gifts and beatitudes they did not know were possible. They discover that this journey was possible only through friendship ... The mission of the Holy Spirit is to move us towards the charity that defines the relationship between the Father and the Son, a charity so full that it is thoroughly one and yet cannot be contained within a single origin or between an original and a copy, but always, eternally, exceeds that relationship into another. The Holy Spirit is that relationship. (D. S. Long, 2001, 302-3)

Long holds that God and *agape* love can become a strategic part of the moral horizon that informs and shapes the self towards a higher plane of flourishing. It can provide a map of sorts. This gives us hope to resolve the problem of the moral gap. Long is optimistic that this will rejuvenate ethics and give new vision and inspiration for moral growth. One's liberation can be found in tapping into a strong source, engaging the higher moral dimensions and richer moral horizon of transcendent goodness. It opens the field of ethics to fresh dialogue and new human potential. We discover that our liberation turns out to be connected to sources of inner motivation.

If philosophical materialism were true to reality, we would not even be discussing the concept of being good, justice or fairness, with or without God, notes American philosopher David Bentley

Hart (2013). We would simply be satisfied to focus on production and reproduction goods. We would not be spending so much time and ink doing moral reflection, or care about our identity, our virtues and vices. This kind of consciousness, this entire discussion would be futile, agrees atheist philosopher Thomas Nagel (*Mind and Cosmos*, 2012). But he asserts that human consciousness and morality needs a proper explanation. Both philosophers seriously question the explanatory power of materialistic naturalism in this regard. Nagel and distinguished philosopher Alvin Plantinga have also been in serious dialogue on this point. Hear what Nagel says.

> The existence of consciousness is both one of the most familiar and one of the most astounding things about the world. No conception of the natural order that does not reveal it as something to be expected can aspire even to the outline of completeness. And if physical science, whatever it may have to say about the origin of life, leaves us necessarily in the dark about consciousness, that shows that it cannot provide the basic form of intelligibility for this world. (T. Nagel, 2012, 53)

Materialistic naturalism lacks the *explanatory range* we need for a more robust kind of reflection about human flourishing.

David Bentley Hart adds fuel to Nagel's pressing concern, pointing out some important internal inconsistencies and contradictions within materialism.

> Naturalism is a picture of the whole of reality that cannot, according to its own intrinsic premises, address the being of the whole; it is a metaphysics of the rejection of metaphysics, a transcendental certainty of the impossibility of transcendent truth, and so requires an act of pure credence logically immune to any verification.... Thus naturalism must forever remain a pure assertion, a pure conviction, a confession of blind assurance in an inaccessible beyond; and that beyond, more paradoxically still, is the beyond of no beyond. (D.B. Hart, 2013, 77)

We have been arguing that God and his love is necessary for our identity, our moral soundness, even the ground of our very being in the world. It speaks to the age-old questions: Why is there something rather than nothing? What is this contingent something (us and the cosmos) grounded in? Hart continues his musings on the amazing personal and cosmic contingency (non self-sufficiency) of our existence. We are radically dependent at a personal, moral, social and cosmological level.

> There is a pure fragility and necessary incompleteness to any finite thing; nothing has its actuality entirely in itself, fully enjoyed in some impregnable present instant, but must always receive itself from beyond itself, and then only by losing itself at the same time. Nothing in the cosmos contains the ground of its own being.... One is contingent through and through, partaking of being rather than generating it out of some source within oneself; and the same is true of the whole intricate web of interdependencies that constitutes nature. (D.B. Hart, 2013, 92-93)

The organizing principle of a human being must come from beyond its own selfhood, beyond its contingent moral and physical existence. A transcendent God as the ultimate source of all things makes sense of the frailty of our existence.

> God alone has necessity in and of himself. That is, if the word "God" has any meaning at all, it must refer to a reality that is not just metaphysically indestructible but necessary in the fullest and most proper sense; it must refer to a reality that is *logically* necessary and that therefore provides the ultimate explanation of all other realities, without need of being explained in turn.... God is absolute being as such, apart from whom nothing else could exist, as either a possibility or an actuality.... It is God's necessity, as the unconditional source of all things that makes any world possible in the first place. (D.B. Hart, 116 and 122)

We have discovered in this journey out of nihilism that there must be an ultimate *source* of the self. Following Charles Taylor's lead to recover the language of the good, there must be a source of empowerment for living in a positive, inspiring relationship to the good, as well as a positive relationship to self. How does *agape* love and divine goodness get translated into human life and society? Our quest moves us out of self-imposed isolation and moral immobility, into interdependency with divine goodness by means of the Holy Spirit. We need a transcendent interface.

For credibility's sake, the good must also become an engaging, embodied, situated *praxis*. It must become incarnational, embedded in social reality, full-blooded, existing in the world, in history. It must be possible for transcendent goodness to be mediated into everyday life, in order to empower us and breathe life into culture. Divine goodness is made present as a *gift* by the Holy Spirit for the formation of the self within community, towards a healthy life narrative. It can also energize scholarship. Take note of Glenn Tinder's fine work (2000), *The Political Meaning of Christianity: an Interpretation,* where he applies *agape* love to a political vision of rights, dignity of the individual and the responsibilities of citizens. Tinder's article in Atlantic Monthly called "Can We Be Good Without God?" hit a chord and went viral. It was equivalent to the first chapter of the above book. Or perhaps we could turn to Jim Wallis' *The (Un)Common Good* (2014), where he applies *agape* love and the principles of *shalom* to social renewal, the common good of society and the world at large, with hope to heal great divisions, tensions and injustices. Both advocate a *prophetic stance* of vulnerable engagement rather than fear and disconnection. Their practical ethical reasoning involves sacrifice and surrender of a domineering self-assertion, coercion, manipulation, prejudice and contempt for others. It is replaced by *agape* love.

The Holy Spirit also offers an accountability mechanism to human attempts to control and manipulate the good for self-interest purposes: for example, to become a sexist, racist or tribal individual or to set up exploitive policies in government. God and transcendent goodness both underwrite and offer checks and balances to human claims to the good. The God's-eye view is not irrelevant after all. The Holy Spirit both grounds and resources the good in the dynamic and superior goodness of a trinitarian God, where there is mutuality of love in relationship. One's individual standard of goodness is no longer the final or ultimate standard, even if one is very powerful or wealthy. It also carries with it a call to humility regarding any claim to, or construction of, the good in family or society. We must hold all human creations of the good lightly and examine them critically.

Such a process of self-constitution opens up the horizon of human moral thinking and action, first towards God, but secondly, connecting the self with human suffering. This *agape* love draws one's life purpose together in compassionate response to others. It deconstructs *responsibility phobia* and narcissism, and that sense of defeat in the face of monumental human need. It motivates one to take enjoyment in sharing responsibility for others, rather than seeing the others as a negative barrier to personal freedom or fulfillment. It empowers the self beyond radical self-interest and individualism, to mature into community service, with sensitivity to the depth and attentiveness to the presence of others in their vulnerability. It calls into question the nihilist paradigm of struggle for maximum power, wealth, or pleasure which costs others dearly.

Theologian Christoph Schwöbel sums up this very significant thought that the good is actualized as a transcendent gift, and as a calling. The quality of our freedom is at stake, freedom that is itself a gift within the confines of God's freedom.

> The reconstitution of created freedom through the appropriation of the revelation of God's goodness in Christ which is made possible in the Spirit is characterized by the acknowledgement of the limitations of human freedom that become evident where this freedom is no longer understood as self-produced, but as a gift of grace. The liberation from the abortive attempt of self-constitution of human freedom discloses the reality of the other person and the non-human creation as the one to whom good action is directed. Human goodness is realized where it is acknowledged that it is not self-produced, but the gift of God's creative, revealing and inspiring action. (C. Schwöbel, 1992, 75)

Through the Holy Spirit, goodness becomes a communicable and accessible daily human possibility and existential reality within the immanent frame. The individual is not left alone to fend for herself, left to her own devices and resources; she does not have to aggressively take what is hers. She does not have to continually self-motivate and self-justify her behavior. Rather, the Holy Spirit reorganizes, reconstitutes, human passions and priorities. This re-connection of human goodness to the transcendent brings a bright hope of retrieving, reviving and sustaining the empowering language of the good and *agape* love as fruitful linguistic currency and powerful, motivating experience. It acts to bridge the moral gap like the Golden Gate Bridge in San Francisco.

Our next move in our great escape beyond nihilism is to grapple with the recovery of the language of *incarnational humanism*, an ancient tradition, one that informs the present as a tremendous cultural dynamo (Jens Zimmermann, 2012a, and 2012b). It will be connected with the concept of *faithful presence* as a style of engagement and leadership within one's world. This will provide the climax of our journey. It will flesh out some of the needed anthropological adjustments we have hinted at thus far, and continue to push towards *fullness* of being and *fullness* of consciousness. As we ascend our mountain, it returns us to a rediscovery of the wonder, gratitude and joy of our existence. We propose a *transcendent turn to incarnational humanism*. We are now going both deeper to the very ground of being, and reaching high for the best human aspirations. By now, we know there must be better way forward.

10

Transcending Nihilism

Incarnational Humanism Offers a Recovery of Our Passion

Intellectual homelessness and personal despair is a very painful and exhausting place to be. So far, we have tunneled out of our prison camp, broken free of a limiting horizon, and ascended beyond the reductionisms and restrictions of nihilism. We have discovered that there is much more to the life of the mind and heart than the idolatries of materialism, scientism and aestheticism are able to bring to the table. They take away our passion. There is much more to life than the Closed World System *spin* allows us to imagine. There is more wisdom, more poetry available to us. We now want to move the discussion onto even higher ground, beginning our ascent, as if circling a mountain towards a fuller human potential, a richer, higher experience of human flourishing.

At the same time, we have to delve deep into the ground of our very existence. We have discovered some things about transcendence, the language of the good, the liberating power of virtue and *agape* love. We are motivated and empowered by the Holy Spirit. We anticipate a richer language, a broader vision, a new culture just over the horizon. Now we want to explore true freedom, robust agency and healthy responsibility, to discover our true passion.

The final section of our discussion is about discovery and articulation of a plausible philosophical and existential home in late modernity, one that is critical to our very survival as a human community. This is no mere intellectual game or power play. Hans Georg Gadamer put it this way:

> The future survival of mankind may depend on our readiness ... to pause in front of the other's otherness – the otherness of nature as well as that of historically grown cultures of peoples and countries.

The courageous journey forward involves a recovery of stable and sustainable purpose, a genuine hope of healing our wounds, and an enhancement of our most precious relationships. To this end, we will attempt to reclaim a critical part of our Western heritage: the *incarnation*. Our location in this quest is the Mount Everest trek Camp Four like the cover of the book. We look up at the last formidable section of the highest mountain in the world. We are living on the edge of an intense accomplishment, nervous about the danger, but awaiting the big reward of a stellar, panoramic view of the world from the summit. Will it bring us to a personal breakthrough? Let us make sure we are roped together and carry extra oxygen tanks in order to sustain our efforts as we press on with the final ascent. We are in search of our very soul, our most intimate inner self (M. Crawford, 2015, 127-95).

Thus far in the journey, we have offered both a protest (*agonisme*) against nihilism and a strategic exit from its shackling grip on our minds and lives. The narrative and its trajectory matters much. Our discussion has demonstrated that we are determined to find meaning in our suffering, to put truth before power, goodness before wealth, honesty and forgiveness before self-justification and masks. Our final ascent involves a transcendent philosophical turn towards *incarnational humanism*. Let us explain how this builds on our previous discussion of *agape* love. It offers an interpretive key to recover a *thick* identity, and win through to a whole new *social imaginary*: the ability to see, interpret and experience reality differently. We can perhaps escape the trap of damaging and restrictive ideologies, in order to include more creativity, more truthfulness, beauty and mindfulness. This kind of humanism has a scholarly reach all the way back to Saint Augustine. It is sourced in the biblical religions, and it is very much alive today. The integrative hermeneutic at hand concurrently provides both a challenge, pushing us to our limits, and an exhilarating basis for inspiration. We are feeling very alive, our imagination is on fire.

The journey begins with a conversation. There is a high degree of resonance with the Creator's dialogue with his creation, despite the contemporary cacophony of conflicting voices. We are addressed, invited to open our hearts and minds to fresh wisdom and self-understanding, to new levels of attentiveness to our divine interlocutor. This communication is writ large in the incarnation. In fact, the incarnation is a great *gift* to humans, God's grand masterpiece. It draws us *upwards* into a new dimension of life, a new caliber of thinking and living. The increased awareness is similar to the way that the Hubble space telescope expands human sight out into 13.8 billion light years of universe with its billions of galaxies and stars. Perseverance and patience are in order if we wish to discover what we came for. We dare not rest until we have captured a full perspective on our new home, one where our hearts can rest with a thrilling sense of peace and ongoing adventure. Thank you for travelling with us this far. We believe that your endurance and thoughtfulness will be rewarded. This has been something of the *Camino de Santiago* reflective walk. We must name our fears and hesitations, and then set them aside in the name of powerful discovery and tangible personal growth. Will we find the Holy Grail?

D. Stephen Long (2009) has made an excellent effort of showing the complexities and nuances of this journey in his *Speaking of God*. This is instructive to the deconstruction of some of our myths and misunderstandings about the compatibility of good faith and clear reasoning. Can reason and faith embrace and complement each other? Clearly, there is a great need to move beyond the hostility, stereotypes and caricatures that are lively in some circles if we are to have fruitful dialogue that garners traction to move us forward.

The incarnation helps us make sense of such things in a more integrated fashion.

> The certainties which the church has received as a gift require its participation in humanity's "common struggle" to attain truth. The human search for truth, which is philosophy's vocation, is not set in opposition to theology's reception of truth as gift. What we struggle to understand by reason we also receive by faith. No dichotomy exists between the certainties of faith and the common struggle by human reason to attain truth.... The truths humanity seeks by common reason (philosophy) and the certainties of faith can be placed over against each other such that each illuminates the other and renders it intelligible until the two ultimately become one, which is of course what the incarnation does in reverse. The concretion of the one Person [the Christ] illumines the natures of both divinity and humanity. (D. S. Long, 2009, 87)

In Christ, amazingly we have both immanence and transcendence, physical and spiritual, earth and heaven. Brilliant UK hermeneutics scholar Anthony Thiselton says that the mystery of the incarnation is too profound for human discovery by reason alone, but requires divine revelation. It is beyond our limited imaginative capture. But open-minded reasoning engages, and is engaged by, such an epiphany. The right posture and intellectual virtues can help us fathom the profound implications of its mutuality. It can change our perception, similar to a paradigm shift.

Addressed by God

Science has not replaced religion, claims Charles Taylor (2007). In fact, we are quite *haunted* by transcendence in our 'secular age'. Humans are addressed by God himself: in the call of Abraham, the burning bush of Moses, or the amazing announcement to teenage Mary. There is a draw upward into a stretching dialogue. We are strongly attracted to reason and commune with our Creator. Individuals are identified as loved, valued, nurtured, embraced and included. These *perlocutionary* events act as a speech act, one that produces an unavoidable impact on the one addressed. He is the one who knows us in our true self, calling us into our fullness, our highest purpose. Hans Urs von Balthasar (R. Gawronski, 1995, *Word and Silence*) sees the Word of God revealed in three rich and powerful ways, three forms of articulation: Creation, Scripture, and the Incarnation. While all these three are different types of speech, each is powerful and laden with meaning. Each offers a robust language usage that complements and is entwined with the others. By their light, we can make sense of the world. Thus, the incarnation has phenomenal explanatory range for late moderns who take time out to listen and reflect. The journey offers a revelation for those who will attend to transcendent speech. As the pinnacle of God's engagement with humanity, the incarnation offers a high call to dialogue.

Alister McFadyen illuminates some important nuances concerning the character of the incarnation. In the incarnation of Jesus of Nazareth, one sees God communicating and relating, not as a tyrannical, coercive, absolute sovereign, but as a vulnerable human individual, a humble suffering servant, as someone who was one of us and knows our pain.

> [By] incarnation in the body of the crucified one implies that God's freedom does not, after all, entail a transcendent aloofness from the world, but a form of involvement with it in which the divine being and freedom are staked. God subjects Godself to the risks, vulnerabilities and ambiguities of historical existence, including the risk of rejection, suffering and death, as well as of misinterpretation. God's freedom and sovereignty must be of a radical kind: the freedom to give oneself in relation; to be with and in creation in ways that are costly to God, but which do not abrogate God's sovereignty, freedom and transcendence. (A. McFadyen, 1995, 42)

This move unites the divine freedom of self-giving *agape* love with the life-world and individual freedom of human beings. Divine love is the most completely free love. In the Christ event, one is confronted with a divine power that is deeply and thoroughly personal and grace-filled, a power in weakness. It consequently has impact through forms of interpersonal communication and personal *presence*. It is not a divine monologue of commands or sayings, but a hospitable dialogue in which humans are attended to, and respected as subjects with a certain limited freedom of choice. They are allowed to ask questions, discern and wrestle with divine speech in creation, scripture and above all the incarnation, Jesus himself.

We remember that the problems of *secularism* actually beckon us to learn from the incarnation. Modernity has hit a wall, as religion and culture scholar Jens Zimmermann notes (*Incarnational Humanism,* 2012a). He argues that a proper Christian focus on the incarnation heads off a host of early and late modern philosophical dead ends, all while stimulating a vision of a robust, recovered humanism. Science was never meant to become a dogma, an *exclusive* humanism. But it is, in fact, a self-limited methodology, a tool, for discovering certain things about the physical dimensions of the world. It always needs a larger context and other layers of meaning in order to function as it should. Unfortunately, science has been *hacked* by the ideology of scientism in the minds of many, and this leads them straight into nihilism, into a deprivation of being.

Even while consciously living in the immanent frame of modernity, we often long for transcendence. Oxford literary scholar C.S. Lewis at one point in his journey came to the end of modernity's game, and mourned that it did not give him the life for which he longed. Rationalism left him feeling dead inside. Materialism left him deflated and bored, showing that this kind of narrow reasoning was insufficient and incomplete. Reason needs love to complete it. Lewis' imaginative explorations in ancient myths helped to revive his mind and his creative imagination. The CBC Ideas presentation on the *Inklings* illustrates this transition in Lewis, this experience of *surprised by joy*. The resulting *Narnia*

Chronicles and *Space Trilogies,* which refused the coldness of nihilism and despair, are now some of the most celebrated literature of all time. Lewis refused to be blind-sided or stifled by scientism. Eventually, he found what he was looking for in a robust Christian faith and humanism, where religion meets culture and animates it, where reason embraces the imagination. This dialogue with God awakens us from our nihilistic, foggy slumber. He has captured our attention. We are strangely moved by divine whisperings. By addressing us in person, God calls us to become beings with different kinds of meaning: culture makers, covenant keepers, gardeners and artisans as well as scientists, technologists and business persons (Andy Crouch, 2008).

The year 2014 marked the hundred-year anniversary of the start of World War I, the conflict that introduced industrial-scale carnage and much painful loss to the world. Never before had science and technology collaborated so effectively to destroy our youth on a mass scale, and in effect disillusion a whole generation. The *Great War* savaged popular beliefs about *progress* through innovation that science had promised to deliver. Yet for two extraordinary authors and friends, J.R.R. Tolkien and C.S. Lewis, this war had a different impact. It deepened their moral and spiritual resolve at a profound level. Both men fought in the trenches on the Western Front and used their experiences, not to succumb to cynicism or give up on civilization, but to shape their Christian imagination.

Actually, they met in the twenties as young scholars at Oxford University and encouraged each other to produce some epic tales. Tolkien wrote *The Hobbit* and *The Lord of the Rings* trilogy. Lewis, who was a strong literary scholar, earned popular fame for *The Chronicles of Narnia,* a series of children's books now considered enduring classics. Both works are now popular movies. These writings have fired the spiritual imagination and opened the hearts of millions around the world. The phenomenon become know at Oxford as the *Inklings,* which also included Charles Williams and

Owen Barfield among others. During the thirties, you might have found them at the Eagle and Child pub discussing their latest work. Dr. John North, English professor at University of Waterloo, delighted to tell stories of how the Tales of Narnia opened up the inner spiritual landscape of his students.

The stories are fundamentally about a cosmic struggle between good and evil—a theme radically out of step with the cynical spirit of the age and our current nihilistic age. Lewis' and Tolkein's use of fantasy captures something of our human predicament, but does not give up hope for humanity itself. New York history Professor Joseph Loconte brilliantly captures this grand narrative of good rescued from evil in *A Hobbit, a Wardrobe, and a Great War* (HarperCollins, 2015).

Many people today sense God calling them to be something more than they presently are, calling them upwards out of their self-pity, consumerism and sullenness. Perhaps they are even called to launch a journey, innovate a solution to a problem, or follow a life-changing quest. Former Archbishop of Canterbury Rowan Williams (2005, 96) asks insightfully, "What makes human life significant, more than animal? Not clothing, not acquisition of coverings for the naked ego, but the conscious participation in an order of compassion." In *The Truce of God*, Williams wants people who have become fearful, disengaged and alienated to take responsibility for their world once again as peacemakers, community builders and servant leaders. Innovative ideas do emerge when we break free from our intense self-absorption, become vulnerable and engage life in good faith. At our best, we are meaning makers, stewards, purpose-oriented. Terrorism, fear, violence and murder are not the last word. Long-term battles are won by the right ideas of fresh alternative strategies.

The *Imago Dei*, God's Icon

The wonder of the incarnation presents humanity with the possibility of full, but finite, personal embodiment of *logos*, the will and wisdom of the divine. As a fleshly, personal wisdom, it sets out an alternative paradigm from self-mastery, self-invention and self-promotion. Jesus is the image (icon) of God that we long for in our honest moments, the most excellent representative of God on earth. He is fully God and fully human. In this way, he provides an exemplar of life lived in the presence of God, offering us an *archetype* of human goodness that is inspired by heaven. Stephen Long (2001) appeals to the *moral normativity* of the life of Jesus, revealing that we are hard wired for such a transcendent relationship.

> In Christian theology, Jesus reveals to us not only who God is but also what it means to be *truly human*. This true humanity is not something we achieve on our own; it comes to us as a gift ... The reception of this gift contains an ineliminable element of mystery that will always require faith. Jesus in his life, teaching, death and resurrection and ongoing presence in the church and through the Holy Spirit ... orders us towards God. He directs our passions and desires towards that which can finally fulfill them and bring us happiness. (D.S. Long, 2001, 106-7)

Transcendent goodness is made present and accessible in the human sphere through the incarnation. It offers us a *transcendent turn* to a new kind of humanism centered in *agape* love. Transcendence of the *strong* variety (C. Schrag, 1997, 110-48) does not mean aloofness or indifference. It is not a burdensome, or unreachable, abstract standard of perfectionism. Rather, it is a creative, palpable engagement with the world, including individuals, society and public institutions. Jesus shows that this goodness can be lived out in the human theatre. The final litmus test of a good moral philosophy is its applicability, its *praxis*.

Jesus provides such an interpretive lens for the human imagination. Although this claim is challenging to grasp, Paul in Colossians 1: 15-20 speaks of Jesus as the source and 'glue' of creation and the purpose or end (*telos*) of creation, both its creative *alpha* and *omega*, beginning and trajectory. He is *above all things* in creation and at the same time the creative basis, the very ground of being. He is that without which nothing would exist, without which this very text would be meaningless. All the *fullness* of God dwells in him. He is God incarnate, in the flesh, fully God and fully man, as the Athanasian tradition states. In him, God's eternity connects with creation's temporality. Paul writes it large: "Jesus is the Yes and Amen to it all" (II Corinthians 1: 18-21). He affirms the human condition while transforming it and setting out new vision for moral capacity in both individual and societal identity.

In his thoughtful book on the subject, J. Richard Middleton (*The Liberating Image,* 2005) claims that Jesus accomplishes all that was anticipated in humans to become a proper regent of God on earth. He faithfully fulfilled this vocation as that strategic representative. Jesus is the complete human, a fullness of humanity, the true *icon* of God. He is the *presence* of God in the world, the *nexus* of the eternal and the temporal. He is a powerful exemplar of divine goodness, to direct our passions and show us the way to live robustly, honestly, humbly and justly. He came to take us higher, out of the murky shadows of our lies, lust for power, addictions and deceptions, and into the *light*. In the popular television program *Scandal*, Olivia Pope the fixer, is hired to save people's reputation in the halls of power in Washington, D.C. She sees so much darkness that at times, she longs to leave it all, quit her job, and step out into the light. Jesus is the reason for this human longing for a noble character and true virtue, for doing the right thing even if it not the easy thing, a longing to remain faithful to one's highest convictions.

He is the fulfillment of all the promises made to the ancient Hebrew patriarchs (Abraham, Isaac, Israel) and the prophetic utterances and longings of the Old Testament, the Jewish Messiah, fulfilling the promise of redemption, renewal, and justice for the poor. Humans have spent much time anticipating someone who could show a better way to do politics, to save us from our own destructive narcissism, violence and vengeance, while teaching us the higher wisdom of God. His life is a unique story, a powerful human narrative of restoration and renewal. The Christ story is the apex of God's compassionate, redemptive interest in humanity.

This demonstrates that we must look beyond mere human flourishing in terms of safety and sustenance, towards the fullest benefit to mankind, towards the *eternal weight of glory*. In the birth, life, teaching, sacrificial death, resurrection and ascension of Jesus Christ, we are offered a new architecture for human potential. His life, care and teaching represent an inspiration, a gripping and tantalizing call to a higher life, a journey up the challenging mountain of moral and spiritual growth. Indeed, it is a symbol of a whole new relationship between humanity and the cosmos. It also poses all sorts of challenging questions to push out the bounds of what it means to be human, to raise the bar, to expand one's identity way beyond the immanent frame, while being extremely relevant to the practical issues of everyday social and political life.

One implication of the incarnation is that Christianity, at its best, is the participation in the life of God and in his presence, a presence as defined by Christ as true and ideal human image bearer. He clears the path to our humanization. More will be said about this later in the subsection on *Suffering Love and a New Community*. Others before him, including Israel as a nation, have tried to measure up to the noble kingly and priestly calling of *Imago Dei*. The incarnation (John 1:1-5, and14; Colossians 1:15-20) in particular provides a vision and a grounding to restore the health of late modern broken relationships, one that can heal us from fragmentation and disenchantment, and pull us back from the abyss. It solves tangible human problems. There is no place for either radical dualism or radical monism under the aegis of the incarnational social imaginary, for it leads us towards holism.

He came to heal and unify humanity, not to fragment it, separate faith and reason, body and spirit, fact and value, natural and supernatural. Incarnation affirms and elevates the whole human in her fullest dimensionality. Jens Zimmermann writes about the robust nature of this image bearing (2012a, 275):

"Bonhoeffer is a Christian humanist because he regards full humanity as the ultimate goal of God's work in Christ." He has much to contribute in his strong scholarly grasp of the rich heritage of Christian humanism, from ancient days to the present. He is also aware of its profound implications for culture wars and the clash of civilizations (J. Zimmerrmann, *Humanism and Religion: a call for the renewal of western culture.* 2012b). Part of our calling is to be transfigured by, and transformed into, the image of Christ. How is that possible?

The Wisdom and Truth of God

Our globalized world can be confusing, even overwhelming given the speed of change, and even frightening with its gruesome international terror networks. We need discernment to learn how to traverse it, and who to trust. The New Testament makes the amazing claim that Jesus is, in the flesh, the wisdom of God and the power of God (I Corinthians 1: 24), the *nexus* and integral relationship of faith and reason. As divine *logos* (John 1: 1-4), he is the transcendent word made flesh, the underwriter of all human thought and language. Truth ultimately is found in a person, a presence, not a mere idea. Jesus is reason personified, the *raison d'être* of it all. The narrative is clear. He is the answer to our deepest questions such as: Why are <u>we</u> here? What is our calling or purpose? Where are we going? Who are we really working for? What do we love? God's speech is embodied, full-blooded, not flat, lifeless or atomistic. The incarnation is a *communicative action* (Kevin Vanhoozer, 2009), so much more than the mere letters, words or sentences. It is loaded with spiritual vitality and meaning: it rings with the poetic, prophetic, and pedagogical.

We are called to seek such wisdom, to take captive all reflection to his Lordship (II Corinthians 10), in other words, his oversight, his scrutiny, to engage his encouragements to think harder and deeper than ever before. He is intensely interested in our ideas and thoughts. He is the *omega point*, the ultimate fulfillment, of every human spiritual, moral and philosophical aspiration to make sense of our existence. He is *public truth*, available to examine by everyone in every faith and ideology, believer and skeptic alike. He offers the "something more", the chance to make sense of the deeper meaning of life itself, revealing its secrets, a window on the river that runs through it. Absence is passé; Jesus is full presence here and now, providing for us a fecundity of existence.

Wisdom shows up as a Hebrew Bible personification in Proverbs 8. Lady wisdom provides a metaphor and a profound motivation for reflection. Heaven knows that we need wisdom today, as a new book by Harvard Professor Eugene Soltes reveals (*Why They Did It: Inside the Mind of the White-Collar Criminal*, 2016). Jesus, as personal wisdom from God, calls out with cautions and enticements to late moderns in the public squares of our towns and globalized mega-cities. People do not need to suffer a shallow, groundless existence, or give up their freedom, reason and identity for a stripped-down materialism or manipulative determinism. Zimmermann's stunning summary insight on this point represents a fresh, gripping re-articulation of reality. It shows that there is something quite profound about the life of Jesus of Nazareth. It is no ordinary life.

> Christ the creative wisdom of God, and God's active Word in creation, is enfleshed in the temporal-historical dimension of our world as the concrete Jewish Messiah, Jesus the Christ.... This is the Word through whom all things were made, and the Word hid in the eternal bosom of God, the Word who spoke through the prophets, the Word whose mighty acts defined the history of Israel. In Jesus the Christ this Word has become flesh, and the eternal has become temporal, but without ceasing to be eternal.... In Christ temporality and eternity are conjoined.... In the incarnation, creation, the world, time and history have been taken up into the God-man, who *is* the center of reality.... Faith and reason are inseparable because their unity is in Christ. (J. Zimmermann, 2012a, 264-5)

Divine poetic language or *speech act* starts with creation: God spoke and the heavens, the stars, the seas, the plants and trees and living creatures, men and women came into existence in abundance. Jesus the Son was there with the Father and the Spirit at creation's dawn, calling it forth into fruitful existence, motivated by love. He is the creative source of all human life, imagination and artistic expression. Divine speech continues in Jesus as the truthful and truth-telling Son of God. As divine word or *logos*, he provides the very architecture of creation. Biology and meta-biology are a whole in Christ. He is God's true revelation, located and embodied truth, claiming that, "If you hold to my teaching, you will be my disciples. Then you will understand the truth and the truth will set you free" (John 8: 31-32). There is power in these words, more for us sojourners than we often imagine. Jesus is the way of wisdom, the way of deep structure integrity. He is the *sign* of something more to the world, the *signifier* of God's great interest in mankind and the *signified*, the goal of all history. Musician Kari Jobe's rendition of the song *Forever* captures something of the breadth and complexity of this insight. We are in dialogue with all this wisdom, all this meaning. What a feast! It has transformative implications to flesh out our lives in surprising ways, to bring us to a breakthrough. It confronts us with the seemingly inescapable question: What will I do with Jesus of Nazareth?

Suffering Love and a New Community

Many people today, children and adults alike, are asking where they fit, how they can discover their passion and make a difference, how they can find a proper mentor and channel their energies. Charles Taylor ("The Self in Moral Space", 1989, 25-52) notes that one key dimension of the moral good is that it is best shaped and carried within community. This is essential to its sustainability, its embodied longevity. King Arthur is nothing without his Camelot. Humans, as created by God in his image (a communal, male-and-female-together concept), have an amazing opportunity for joyful collaboration. But clearly, it does not always work that way.

Sometimes, there is terrible division and rivalry, alienation and conflict, scapegoating and even murder of the innocents. We often want others to suffer for us, we use them illicitly and project our blame on them. Some dictators make their whole citizenship pay a high cost, in order to maintain power.

Beyond Jesus' profound bodily presence on earth, he has also been present in his community (John 14-17; Ephesians 4). As *agape* love incarnate, he left a following to carry the vision forward, and he commissioned a mentored leadership—the Apostles. This community is a historical extension of the incarnation. This diverse, worldwide community of Christians (now around two billion) offers a cultural presence, performance and embodiment of God's goodness, an influence of *salt and light* conscience for society, socially locating divine goodness (*agape* love) in diverse places around the globe and having some profound influence for the good. This entails a tremendous responsibility, and benefit, for humankind at large. Its concern is the flourishing of all, including a profound commitment to dialogue across various traditions and promote peace (M. Volf, 2015).

Tübingen theologian Christoph Schwöbel (1992, 76) notes that divine goodness, a communion of love, "finds its social form in the community of believers as the reconstituted form of life of created and redeemed sociality." The point is that this community is called to communicate, mediate, and live into their baptism, live into divine goodness. They are called to promote the virtues of charity, humility, reconciliation and mercy as a redeeming influence on social governance. The ethics of 'conquer or be conquered' is not the last word. Through this contemporary living incarnation, average people are invited to become entrepreneurs of the abundant goodness of God in the places that they inhabit (*sitz im leben*). Goodness operates at a deeper depth than suffering and evil and helps people get perspective on their pain. This international community welcomes the challenge to engage human brokenness, without becoming crushed by it. They are challenged but not overwhelmed.

Goodness is no idealistic fantasy, because it is empowered in the human theatre and human relationships through this accessible connection to transcendent goodness, as we spoke about in Chapter 9. This aspect of the incarnation is a profound sign that God has invited humans into communion with the holy Trinity. This communion offers a ground for the mutuality of social being itself, the basic framework of human community. In this sense, Jesus is the hermeneutic of a new, reconciled humanity, drawn from all the nations, religions and ideologies of the globe, inviting us to climb up the mountain to higher existential ground. This high calling of suffering love is promoting a new way of seeing life on planet earth, the way of becoming renewed people in communities, small and large. It provides the conditions for the plausibility of resurrection life.

> A call is not an impersonal cause that makes something happen in a mechanical way.... Call comes in our ears, beckoning us into the future, bringing us into a way of life that has never been experienced in just this way before: a promise, a new thing, a blessing, our place in the new creation, a resurrection life. (E. Peterson, 2010, 34)

It is a call to a new humanity committed to practice forgiveness and make peace, to show compassion, to become a life-giving presence, a sacrament of grace.

We find ourselves climbing this Everest, sustained by grace, onwards to maturity. When we stretch ourselves in this way, we quickly identify cumbersome baggage that we can shed for the higher goal. There is some soreness of muscles and shortness of breath and the air may be a bit thin. It looks tough, but we are not alone. We feel the power of its draw on us. In community, roped together, we work together as a team, receive gifts from others and learn how to share our giftedness. Christian community is profoundly all about gift and grace from beginning to end. These gifts, this transcendent economy of giftedness, makes life rich and meaningful, surprising and delightful (C. Schrag, 1997, 139-143). It engages us at the various interfaces of our lives. As we gear up, we bravely face the largeness of the task ahead, the immensity and inspiration of a *now and future world*. We are relentless.

The chaos, bigotry and greed within our global theatre inspire us to action, to use our giftedness for the benefit of others. Contrast this to minimalist, reductionist ethics of nihilism.

> We depersonalize God to an idea to be discussed. We reduce people around us to resources to be used. We define ourselves as consumers to be satisfied. The more we do it, the more we incapacitate ourselves from growing up to a maturity capable of living adult lives of love, adoration, trust and sacrifice.... In our identity-confused society, too many of us have settled for a pastiche identity composed of social security number, medical records, academic degrees, job history, and whatever fragments of genealogy we can salvage. (E. Peterson 2010, 66, 79)

Within this incarnational community of compassion, human suffering and alienation can be taken seriously and dealt with through communal care. Jesus of Nazareth accepted the mandate of the *Suffering Servant* spoken of by Isaiah the 8th century BCE prophet. He is the servant who empathizes with our human vulnerabilities. He does not stand far off, but is the servant who suffers while protesting against the way things stand. The call of Abraham and of Israel was to become a blessing to all tribes, all nations. Jesus associates with the strange, lonely and exiled. Jimmy Myers captures it beautifully.

> [Jesus] exemplifies and creates a people committed to what David Hart calls 'strange, impractical, altogether unworldly tenderness' to those whom Nietzsche would have annihilated.... The beauty of this person, wholly man and wholly God, lies in the mystery that he brings salvation to the world not by excluding suffering but by uniting himself to it. (J. Myers, *First Things*, 2015)

Jesus' compassion provides moral spine as an exemplar for the incarnational community, and for the larger human community. He models and mentors us in the virtues and the graces of a courageous new world. At the end of his life, Nietzsche (*Dionysus Versus the Crucified*) realized that it came down to a choice between the Christ (suffering love) and Dionysus (self-interest and godlike entitlement). He despised Christian *agape* love and the vulnerable concern for the victim. Late moderns would be wise to ponder the consequences of such a choice, as they continue to stare into their own personal abyss.

> [Jesus] brings the whole festival of divine grace to a world that has excluded itself from it and invites…humanity to take part, to enjoy a feast of resurrection where all divisions, segregation, and exclusion are transcended, where all have their place at the supper of the Lamb, where all, who see the face of the Beautiful One and in that seeing are transformed, are inundated and radiated by Beauty itself. In a word, to paraphrase St. Athanasius, he becomes the Ugly One so that we, the original ugly ones who have made this world ugly with our violence, might become beautiful. (J. Myers, *First Things,* 2015)

This is truly a shocking statement. Jesus' suffering is not weak, frustrating or pathetic, but a highly effective, healing, redemptive love. He brings to an end the human obsession with sacrifices and scapegoating behavior (René Girard, 1978 and 2012). He breaks the back of evil and helps to expose its dark mechanisms, deceptions and tactics. He is the ultimate victim to end all victimization and violence against the neighbor, stranger, against another race or religion.

Entailed in this compassion, Jesus is also a sign of anger against exploitation, victimization, marginalization and injustice. In fact, all prophetic traditions have been concerned with justice. He is intolerant of evil and cruelty, opposing ideals, institutions and structures that seek to undermine human flourishing and seek to exploit others for personal gain, or ignore the needs of the poor and vulnerable. Moreover, he is against politicizing religion, against using public rage for the purpose of controlling the masses or winning votes. David Hart (2009) makes an excellent case for the transformative power of Christian love in shaping history. This *agape* community provides a *home* (Luke 6), a safe refuge amidst the challenges, conflicts, tragedies, and transitions of life. It addresses directly the pressures from the tectonic issues of our globalized world—inequity, xenophobia, war refugees, climate concerns, national debt, and terrorism.

The *agape* community offers a space where we can become *persons* and find freedom. It offers hermeneutical capacity to exegete life differently, provide motivation for reconciliation. "Peace does not come without integrity, wholeness of human desire." (R. Williams, 2005, 103). Incarnate communal life releases us from unconscious fear, anxiety, defensiveness and the ingrained compulsions of rivalry. We recover the art of contemplation: awareness of our vulnerability, interdependence, contingency and humility in the presence of the other.

The teaching in the Sermon on the Mount offers the world a kind of Magna Carta, a bright source of hope. Indian statesman Mahatma Gandhi was impressed with its force, even though he never became a Christian. American social activist Jim Wallis brings a very this-worldly, cultural exposition to this transcendent teaching in his passionate reflection *The (Un)Common Good* (2014). It offers a foundation for mature leadership.

> When Jesus is asked by his disciples who will be first in his kingdom, he tells them it will be the servants of all. Humility is one of the most poorly appreciated values in our intensely competitive culture, economy and politics. (J. Wallis, 2014, 49).

Jesus followers, at their most authentic, do not accept injustice and violence, oppression and exploitation, racism, imperialism, privileging of the beautiful, the rich and the powerful. For example, the United Nations International Charter of Human Rights is a landmark statement on the value of each human being and how they ought to be treated.

Charles Malik, President of the UN General Assembly, was a key player in drafting the document and getting a majority of nations to sign. He was motivated by his Christian faith and his concern for justice and peace in the world after a very destructive World War II. Jesus followers interrupt the victimization of others and call the aggressors out on their bullying tactics (M. Volf, *Exclusion and Embrace*, 1996). They do not promote or tolerate social chaos and anarchy. Instead, they carve out a redemptive path. An example of this courageous stance is the *Truth and Reconciliation Commission* in both South Africa and Rwanda. Dr. Martin Luther King Jr., who saw how mutual love could empower social change and call us to our best, understood the critical testimony of the 'Beloved Community', which is rooted in the ethics of the Sermon on the Mount. Suffering love, as we see in the feature film *Selma*, came from a deep, compassionate, non-violent faith base. It empowered King and his colleagues daily. He continually called people to the mountaintop of virtue, reconciliation and justice. We need his dream today.

One key historical landmark for the beloved community is the resurrection. Former UK Bishop and public intellectual Lesslie Newbigin called it a *singularity*, something that cannot be explained by anything prior, a brilliant new hope for change, a cultural breakthrough. Eugene Peterson (*Practice Resurrection*, 2010) writes on growing up into maturity in Christ using the theme and metaphor of resurrection. Andy Crouch is our creditor as he captures the impact.

> The resurrection was a culture-shaping event.... If indeed it happened as Jesus' followers proclaimed, [it] changed more of subsequent human history, for more people and more cultures, than any other event one can name... The resurrection of Jesus is like a cultural earthquake, its epicenter located in Jerusalem in the early 30's [C.E.], whose aftershocks are being felt in the cultural practices of people all over the world, many of whom have never heard of, and many more of whom have never believed in, its

> origins.... The resurrection is the hinge of history–still after two thousand years as culturally far-reaching in its effects as anything that has come since.... It is a cultural triumph–an answer, right in the midst of human history, to all the fears of Israel in the face of its enemies.... Indeed one of the most dramatic cultural effects of the resurrection is the transformation of that heinous cultural artifact known as a cross. An instrument of domination and condemnation becomes a symbol of the kingdom that Jesus proclaimed; an alternative culture where grace and forgiveness are the last word.... The cross, the worst that culture can do, is transformed into a sign of the kingdom of God–the realm of forgiveness, mercy, love and indestructible life. (A. Crouch, 2008, 143, 145, 146)

The incarnation is truly a game changer regarding how we discover our individuality and our passion, and the posture from which we attend to reality. Within the outlook of moral-communal inclusiveness, our perspective is altered significantly. We repost Taylor's grid of the self, to show that the social dimension (Category B) is taken more seriously, and category A (iii) is more about the reform of society within the hermeneutic of incarnational humanism. A. McFadyen (1995) offers a clarifying reflection concerning the distortions of the popular myth of the radically autonomous individual, and unqualified choice.

> The free pursuit of private self-interest has a naturally conflicting form, since the otherness of the individual means their interests must be opposed. One needs freedom from what is other in order to be oneself. Personal centeredness is essential, for autonomy is a private place that has to be protected by fencing it off from the sphere of relation and therefore from the otherness of God and one's neighbors ... Autonomy is something one has in self-possession, apart from relation to God and others in an exclusive and private orientation on an asocial personal center ... Freedom and autonomy are had apart from relationship: they inhere within oneself. (A. McFadyen, 1995, 35)

Noted German sociologist Jürgen Habermas problematizes this contemporary preoccupation in the West with the autonomy and self-mastery, which we also see in Foucault and many other poststructuralist philosophers. He shows that it is not in touch with key existential realities.

> Both cognitive-instrumental mastery of an objective nature (and society) and a narcissistically overinflated autonomy (in the sense of purposively rational self-assertion) are derivative moments that have been rendered independent from the communicative structures of the lifeworld, that is, from the intersubjectivity of relationships of mutual understanding and relationships of reciprocal recognition. (J. Habermas, 1987, 315)

Habermas suggests that we need to mature beyond the fantasy of our radical individualism in order to grow up into adulthood. This is on the same trajectory of a new identity within the plausibility structure of incarnational humanism. There is no conflict of interest or contradiction in this scenario.

We are indeed capable of living alternative lifestyles, ones that are rooted in contemplation, compassion, receptivity, responsiveness to the aspirations and needs of others. The mutual respect of collaboration, cooperation and complementarity subverts fear, mistrust, and tribalism. It reduces violence as we seek new and fruitful ways of being human together. "At its center and permeating its relationships is the conviction that truth can only be shown and spoken in compassion—attention to the other, respect for and delight in the other, and also willingness to receive loving attention in return" (R. Williams, 2005, 123). This shows up in Taylor's chart below in Category B, social and moral accountability. This perspective can handle difference, diversity, and plurality without fragmentation or ghettoization. It can help mitigate the centrifugal forces of contemporary life, providing a center that can hold. The alternative is just too frightening and destructive to consider.

Taylor's Moral Self-Construction Diagnostics

Category A (*Creativity*)

(i) Creation and construction (as well as discovery) of the self.

(ii) Pursuit of originality in one's self-crafting.

(iii) Opposition to the rules of society and even potentially to what one recognizes as morality, or the moral order.

Category B (*Social and Moral Accountability*)

(i) Openness to horizons of significance prevents one's self-creation from losing the background that can save one from insignificance and trivialization (self-destruction of meaning).

(ii) Self-definition needs to be developed in dialogue with significant others, that is, fellow moral interlocutors within a community and a narrative. (Taylor, 1991, 65, 66)

Leadership for a Brave New World

In the movie *Invictus,* Nelson Mandela wisely displays the insight that positive social change must begin with a different sense of identity, one of belonging to the other. The ability of people of different races and interests to imagine their common destiny is key to breaking down racial barriers and healing resentments erected during the Apartheid era in South Africa. Mandela offered a vision of a new humanism and won the world's admiration for his heroic efforts to reunite the country and redress terrible imbalances, racial tension and injustice. Many religious leaders and believers supported this vision. Incarnational humanism has such a vision to renegotiate relationships in late modernity, offering a new set of power relations. We have also constructed the stage for a new posture in life, a new storyline for fullness of mutual flourishing.

The incarnation is all about presence rather than absence. With this kind of humanism in mind, we want to explore the dynamics of what renowned University of Virginia sociologist James Davison Hunter calls *faithful presence* (J.D. Hunter, 2010, 238-54). Because of our journey thus far, we resonate with his project for social change and his mandate for servant leadership. It extends the concept of suffering service to others, with deep relevance to the common good. We should listen as Hunter emphasizes the urgency in our cultural situation.

> Without a commitment to ideals that transcend the self and that direct life beyond self-interest, one is left with a despair that is not only joyless but also is indifferent towards need and thus incapable of addressing need. Hope is intimately tied to beauty for it is images of beauty and loveliness that inspire imagination and expand human possibility. (J.D. Hunter, 2010, 263)

Under the banner of incarnational humanism, faithful presence offers a way to credibly re-articulate the narrative journey of self within late modernity, to find its new home beyond the barbed wire of war, hate and control, will to power nihilism. We use this language of *presence* to communicate this important concept of closeness to the divine. For example, the entire biblical message is the offer of life marked by goodness, peace, truth, beauty, joy, fruitfulness—*shalom*. Hunter writes that *shalom* also offers something serious to society at large, and it would be astute for the incarnational community to pay attention to his voice. This is a robust sense of being with others, taking responsibility for the other.

> A vision of order and harmony, fruitfulness and abundance, wholeness, beauty, joy and well-being.... Christians are to live toward the well-being of others, not just to those in the community of faith, but to all. (J.D. Hunter, 2010, 228 and 230).

The *shalom* of God entails the *presence* of God (Ephesians 2:14) in the world. Incarnational community means that followers of Jesus are mandated to be and bring this *faithful presence,* this incarnational kind of humanism to their circle of influence, to everyday work and social life. Humans can be fully present to each other within the community of faith and fully present to those who are not at the moment part of that community. We pursue each other, identify with each other, and direct our lives towards mutual flourishing.

> Pursuit, identification, the offer of life through sacrificial love—this is what God's faithful presence means. It is a quality of commitment that is active, not passive; intentional, not accidental; covenantal, not contractual. In the life of Christ, we see how it entailed his complete attention. It was a whole-hearted, not half-hearted; focused and purposeful, nothing desultory about it. His very name, Immanuel, signifies all of this—"God with us"—in our presence. (J.D. Hunter, 2010, 243)

Faithful presence is an Everest quality ascent. People who carry this vision are creating structures that incarnate wellbeing, beauty, and purpose. This includes former cynics, secularists, anarchists and nihilists, rich and poor. We claim this incarnational posture as a different kind of plausibility structure. Hunter sharpens the point of faithful presence as it passes through a new prism.

> I have argued that there is a different foundation for reality and thus a different kind of binding commitment symbolized most powerfully in the incarnation. The incarnation represents an alternative way by which word and world come together. It is in the incarnation and the particular way the Word became incarnate in Jesus Christ that we find the only adequate reply to the challenges of dissolution and difference. If, indeed, there is a hope or an imaginable prospect for human flourishing in the contemporary world, it begins when the Word of shalom becomes flesh in us and is enacted through us toward those with whom we live, in the tasks we are given, and in the spheres of influence in which we operate. When the Word of all flourishing—defined by the love of Christ—becomes flesh in us, in our relations with others, within the tasks we are given, and within our spheres of influence—absence gives way to presence, and the word we speak to each other and to the world becomes authentic and trustworthy. (J.D. Hunter, 2010, 252)

The practice of faithful presence is the incarnation of a fresh and constructive kind of servant leadership and mentorship (Robert K. Greenleaf, 1998; Don Page, 2009) in all realms of life, all careers, all human endeavors. Don Page, former speechwriter for the Prime Minister of Canada, and Professor Emeritus at Trinity Western University in their Masters Program in Leadership, made a substantial contribution to servant leader culture internationally. It simply makes sense that offering dignity and respect for employees creates a better work environment and a more successful company, NGO or non-profit agency. It creates significant opportunities and space for others to participate and develop, championing their giftedness, creativity and potential. His work is literally changing the world, changing values in the workplace. It resonates with Hunter's faithful presence.

> The practice of faithful presence generates relationships and institutions that are covenantal. These create space that fosters meaning, purpose, and belonging and by so doing these relationships and institutions resist the instrumentalization endemic to the modern world that tends to reduce the value of people and the worth of creation to mere utility, whether utility is oriented to market efficiency, expanding power, or personal fulfillment.... To provide for the physical, aesthetic, intellectual, and social health of the community is a good in its own right. (J.D. Hunter, 2010, 266)

Below are some striking examples of how this concept of faithful presence can be exercised. It can often start with just one person who takes the incarnation vision seriously and begins to live sacrificially and faithfully. One inspired person who wants to live out servant leadership is all it takes to begin a movement for the common good. Rowan Williams spoke of the Taizé Ecumenical Community in Burgundy, France. They have had an enormous influence, and have captured the imagination of many European youth who wanted to engage the world constructively. Taizé has ambassadorial cell groups living among the poor in Asia, Africa and Latin America. This effort towards integral relationships amidst difference "represents a serious political concern, an eagerness to listen and learn across cultural boundaries, a sensitivity for certain styles in art and liturgy, traditional but spare and contemporary in expression, a profoundly contemplative spirituality" (R. Williams, 2005, 124). There are many more.

Hunter mentions a group in the state of Michigan, hit hard by the recent Great Recession of 2008, who build not-for-profit housing to address the scourge of poverty and homelessness. A friend of ours mentioned a company that subsidized solar panels for poor areas and trained people in installing these for others. The Mennonite Central Committee sponsors a store called *Ten Thousand Villages* with low overhead to assist talented artisans in developing countries to sell their work in the West, promoting *shalom* in both contexts. People on campus are captivated by the joy and creativity in this program. Character Canada is an organization in Abbotsford, British Columbia, Canada, started by Fran Vanderpol. This organization rallies the whole community (police, educators, city hall, and other community organizations) to promote good citizenship and the virtues of noble character. It is having a great impact through annual conferences and local networks. David Brooks brings this vision of recovering character to the fore in his important contribution *The Road to Character* (2015).

Servant leadership with courage, depth and grace comes from Katherine Hayhoe, a climate scientist from Texas, who has demonstrated incredible patience with climate change deniers. She has pursued with exceptional persistence her message of care for the future of our biosphere and our grandchildren in the human community. She was once featured in *Time Magazine* as one of the hundred most influential women. We value a colleague who is an advocate for healing relations with Native Canadians. His patient listening care incarnates *agape* love and inspires many others to participate in this dialogue. Susan Cain's (2012) research on the power of introverts is instructive in this constructive leadership.

Jim Wallis, a social compassion expert of Sojourners Community fame, has put in endless hours building bridges and promoting justice though lobbying government and neighbourhood compassion work, outreach to the poor and marginalized, healing political fragmentation and promoting the common good of society. There are many others who are finding deep meaning in helping others, in creating a new social *ethos*. Like Buckminster Fuller, they want 'a world that works for everyone.'

Below are ten commitments from Jim Wallis to suggest how one can be a faithful presence in family, society and work towards the common good (J. Wallis, *The (Un)Common Good,* 2014, 297-98). At the end of the day, we must make key decisions, set strategic priorities, take responsibility for our world, and invest wisely in the future. We believe that discovery of this integral relationship between our own personal interests and those of others (the common good) is our best chance in late modernity for a brave new world of unity amidst diversity, to promote a center that holds. It is the best chance to master this summit of Everest morally, spiritually, ethically and politically. It is a strong hope that we hold out for a better tomorrow as a human community, a new economy of relationships. This is what we want to bring to the table of discussion, dialogue and debate in late modernity. Please examine the inner merits of the position and put it to the test. It is not enough to interrogate and escape from nihilism, violence and anti-humanism. We must carve out a new space to be fully human, set new priorities, plant new crops, develop new habits and precedents for a new philosophy of life. It can become our new home, a new place to rest our hearts, to discover passion, joy and meaning in life. We believe that it is our best hope to find our voice and to help others find theirs, the way of wisdom.

Ten Personal Decisions for the Common Good

Jim Wallis

1. If you are a father or a mother, make your children the most important priority in your life and build your other commitments around them. If you are not a parent, look for children who could benefit from your investment in their lives.

2. If you are married, be faithful to your spouse. Demonstrate your commitment with both your fidelity and your love. If you are single, measure your relationships by their integrity not their usefulness.

3. If you are a person of faith, focus on not just what you believe but on how you act on those beliefs. If you love God, ask God how to love your neighbor.

4. Take the place you live seriously. Make the context of your life and work the parish that you take responsibility for.

5. Seek to develop a vocation and not just a career. Discern your gifts as a child of God not just your talents, and listen for your calling rather than just looking for opportunities. Remember that your personal good always relates to the common good.

6. Make choices by distinguishing between wants and needs. Choose what is enough rather what is possible to get. Replace appetites with values, teach your children the same, and model those values for all who are in your life.

7. Look at the business, company, or organization where you work from an ethical perspective. Ask what its vocation is too. Challenge whatever is dishonest or exploitive and help your place of employment do well by doing good.

8. Ask yourself what in the world today most breaks your heart and offends your sense of justice. Decide to help to change that and join with others who are committed to transform that injustice.

9. Get to know who your political representatives are at both a local and national level. Study their policy decisions and examine their moral compass and public leadership. Make your public convictions and commitments known to them and choose to hold them accountable.

10. Since the difference between events and movements is sacrifice, which is also the true meaning of religion, and what makes for social change, ask yourself what is important enough to give your life to and for.

Jim Wallis (2014, 297-8) used with permission from Brazos Press, a division of Baker Publishing Group.

Conclusion

The irony of late modernity is that, just when we thought we were most fully free, we discovered that we were actually most in chains. We dare to know the truth about our situation, and to think critically about it. We also long to experience life in its fullness and abundance, to live with passion. We want to discover our calling and make a meaningful contribution. We have discovered that nihilism is a seductive trap, with false promises that cannot deliver. Radical individualism is out of touch with reality, it does not sustain, and cynicism self-destructs. Nihilism leaves us homeless, fearful, deceptive, suspicious, isolated, and morally frozen. Ultimately, it is a form of anti-humanism, working against our best interests, as well as the best interests of others. The great escape from nihilism, as we have articulated it, is a committed process. It moves us out of naïveté into maturity. We have been on a *spiritual* journey that requires both map (a new paradigm) and compass (wisdom, discernment, interpretive skill). We do have the choice of a robust alternative, an upward trek towards virtue, which is at the heart of human flourishing. With some help, we can recover a fresh consciousness, an effective individuality in relation to the good, to *agape* love, and to community. We can live from the depth of character, rather than stroll superficially as *flâneurs*, aristocrats of style, or reduce ourselves to technical performers, a mere cog in the big economic machinery.

We have committed ourselves to follow a promising hermeneutic of the good, to see where it takes us. We have chosen to pursue and promote the good, the true and the beautiful even amidst much evil, deception, and reality distortion. The good informs, roots and contextualizes the self, strengthens its agency, and transforms it through a transcendent turn towards *agape* love. The good gives content and direction to choice and freedom, in order to rescue it from some of its most negative, antisocial possibilities.

The good helps late modern cultural refugees make a new home, one where faith and reason work together in a mutually fruitful way. It helps us recover a healthy social horizon informed by creativity, compassion and collaboration. Autonomy is modified by mutuality and *I-Thou* relationship. We discover the social body, the communal dimension of individuality and subjectivity. We pursue dialogue for deeper truth and common ground amidst people of difference and plurality. We reject incommensurability of cultures and we open dialogue on matters of significance, things that concern us all. We look for the good in others, affirm it and seek to draw it out, build on it. We also seek to name, expose and restrain evil and corruption. The hermeneutic of the good, and its incarnational humanism, involves a recovery of the language and horizon of the moral good, the social horizon of the neighbor, and the theological horizon of transcendent trinitarian goodness. It is robust, creative and revelatory. It produces a whole new narrative to address the current crisis of self, and the crises of society.

A New Sense of Call

This has been a charged journey in search of freedom within a deeper calling that involves the creativity of interdependencies and complementarities. We have moved well beyond cynicism and disenchantment, the obsession with self-fulfillment and self-justification. We have escaped the trap of extreme self-reflexivity. The future is open to involve integral thinking, problem solving, pursuit of unity amidst plurality, reconciliation and forgiveness, principled diplomacy, equity of opportunity and peacemaking. The posture has moved us from self-assertion to humble servant leadership and hospitality, from pure self-interest to a welcomed responsibility for others, from the isolation of aloofness and indifference to vulnerability and trust. The worthwhile pursuit and practice of such virtues builds a solid ground for freedom with depth, freedom in the long run. This calling celebrates the anatomy of the virtuous community: including covenant and commitment, one another attitude, mentorship, servant leadership and use of one's gifts for the other and for the common good.

Religion can no longer be seen as either irrelevant or a pure threat in late modernity. Many will continue to exploit religion for power purposes, but this is not seen as legitimate or helpful. With proper discernment (M. Volf, 2015; J. Sacks, 2002), religion of the right sort can add much to a vision for human flourishing in an age of globalization and late capitalism. Religion binds people together, and speaks to their dignity, the power of the human spirit. It is an explanation of who we are and why we exist beyond food, clothing and recreation. *Homo sapiens,* empirically and historically, is the meaning seeking animal. We sense instinctively that we are more than simply producers and consumers, more than a house, a career and a bank account. We want *more* from life and that means re-connecting to the transcendent.

So we have stepped back from the abyss of despair and discovered in the incarnation a new transcendent-immanent horizon of meaning, a powerful new plausibility structure. We have recovered an empirically honest human anthropology, which is also more hopeful in its potential for individual and social change. This empowers one to love self, the world, the other and God, to recognize hopeful signs. Repressed goods re-appear, equipped to empower agency for healthy debate and social engagement. After atheism and hardcore secularism, we find a new ground for rights, respect, wellbeing and justice for all, not just for the few or the loud. We have discovered that Jesus' life interprets freedom differently—it is thoroughly qualified by transcendent goodness. It is all about relationship, not about absence but rather presence, attentiveness, vulnerability, wholeheartedness. It is a creative way of being present with others: in creative recognition of their autonomy within the relationship. It creates space for more being. Individual identity is strengthened and thickened through generosity, gratitude and mutuality.

Christoph Schwöbel (1995) captures this concept. Freedom as he sees it is truly a gift from God, rooted in the character of God as trinity.

> [It is in the] Image of Christ, where freedom is exercised as rooted in the will of the Father and mediated in the power of the Spirit that the true character of the image of God is disclosed to us, both as the divine freedom for grace and as the human freedom of obedience.... Christ is ... both the revelation of the divine freedom of grace and the disclosure of the human freedom of obedience, where obedience to the will of God the father is not the abrogation of human freedom but the form of its exercise. (C. Schwöbel, 1995, 80)

In the incarnation, one sees God communicating and relating, not as a tyrannical, coercive, absolute sovereign, a view that many have rejected today. Rather God has acted vulnerably in and through the form of a human individual, by uniting the divine freedom of self-giving *agape* love with the agency of a human being, acting in a community, within a historical-cultural context. In the Christ event, one is confronted with the highly personal, which consequently has impact through forms of interpersonal communication and personal presence. This God posture makes creative appeal to human freedom. It is not a divine monologue of commands, but a dialogue in which humans are intended and respected as subjects with choice. Human freedom must be read against the backdrop, and within the horizon of, God's freedom as revealed in the incarnation, the greatest work of art of all time. It is the foundation of a renewed humanism called *shalom*.

Freedom, its content and definition, has been an underlying theme in this book. But we need both negative and positive freedom. When freedom embraces goodness, it transforms freedom from an end in itself, to freedom as a benevolence. Within the plausibility structure of trinitarian transcendent goodness, *agape* love becomes the content of freedom as well as freedom's trajectory. Such redeemed freedom takes seriously the human and divine other, especially the weaker, more vulnerable human other. This redirected, redeemed freedom is a consequence of the link between human and divine goodness. Schwöbel captures it succinctly.

> The true measure of freedom is love as the relationship, which makes the flourishing of the other the condition of self-fulfilment. Human freedom becomes the icon of divine freedom where the freedom of divine grace constitutes the grace of human freedom ... That most poignant image of hope, the Kingdom of God, expresses the relation of free divine love and loving human freedom together in depicting the ultimate purpose of God's action as the perfected community of love with his creation. The fulfillment of God's reign and the salvation of creation are actualized together in the community of the love of God. (C. Schwöbel, 1995, 80-81)

At the end of the day, we are not part of a secular age, but rather an age of discovery and personal growth. We ascend this mountain to get perspective on life. We no longer ask Why am I here? Instead, we ask How can I help? The myth of *nihilism* is a self-con we late moderns have perpetrated upon ourselves. We do not actually want materialistic or deterministic restrictions, or implosion of the religious and ethical into the aesthetic. We want fullness of being, high virtues to shape us, and robust social networks to sustain us and promote just relations for a better world, a less violent and more creative future. This has been shown to be eminently possible in our time, as it has in ancient times. Our final challenge is to choose freedom, choose the good and responsibility, to choose *agape* love as a solid grounding of life, a deep empowerment to direct our energies and rediscovering our passion in late modernity.

A Personal Note to Christian Graduate Students

What are the implications of the incarnation for our identity, our posture and our voice on campus? Incarnation is "where God's eternity and creation's temporality meet" (D. S. Long, 2009, 86). This is no simplistic postulation, but it is great territory to explore, good soil for fruitful study and personal reflection. If indeed Jesus is the wisdom of God and the power of God, the reason, the *telos* or goal of everything (Colossians 1), it would be terribly wrong to keep this a secret from our colleagues and friends. If we are able to say 'Jesus is Lord' with respect to our studies, our lives and our relationships (Romans chapters 8 and 12), that will begin to transform us and give us fresh motivation, creativity and joy. It will take a lifetime to explore its implications to the full, but graduate school is a good place to start. We need wisdom and endurance every day to discern our research. Wisdom as articulated in the Proverbs is an intensely practical method of thinking and living more fruitfully. The cultivation of wisdom is continuously a valuable quest in all arenas of life.

We have been on a journey in this discussion to escape from nihilism's grip, and now to discover our passion and re-settle our priorities in a more mysterious, beautiful and adventure filled world. Creation is the first and last word in the Bible and it is grounded in love. It is God's creation and his renewal of creation that fascinates—a new heaven and a new earth is promised in John's Revelation. We are called to climb this mountain, with full view of the virtues in front of us, while climbing the academic and career ladder. Our goal, over several decades, in Graduate Christian Union and the Graduate and Faculty Christian Forum at UBC, plus our wider network, has been to support and inspire the vision of graduate students. Many have gone on to great accomplishments while taking their faith seriously. They held onto their university ideals and carried the vision forward. They held on to both faith and reason. Now the baton is passed to you as current graduate students. Test these ideas and claims, extend the concepts, run the experiment and become an entrepreneur of meaningful dialogue, character depth and strategic action. We are called to think and read deeply and widely. Find wise people to mentor you and wear out their doorstep, whether through reading their books or personal contact. It is also important to look for someone to mentor in agape love and incarnational humanism. Reflect often on what is good, excellent and praiseworthy. Live without shame, live vulnerably and wholeheartedly. Seek out joy and live with gratitude for the unique gift that is your daily opportunity. Learn the art of hospitality and become a great and generous soul like Dr. Hill, a faithful presence in your circle of influence, and a promoter of shalom. Go the extra mile in all your relationships, pursue the good and do the right thing, even if it is sometimes the hardest thing.

Bibliography

Abbey, R. (2000). *Charles Taylor*. Teddington, UK: Acumen.

Alexander, D. (2001). *Rebuilding the Matrix: science and faith in the 21st century*. Grand Rapids, MI: Zondervan.

Anderson, W.T. (1997). *The Future of the Self: exploring the post-identity society*. New York, NY: Penguin.

Berger, P. & T. Luckman (1967). *The Social Construction of Reality: a treatise on the sociology of knowledge*. New York, NY: Anchor Books.

Bloom, A. (1989). *The Closing of the American Mind: How Higher Education Has Failed Democracy and Empoverished the Souls of Students*. New York, NY: Simon and Schuster.

Bouma-Prediger, S. (2010). *For the Beauty of the Earth: a Christian vision of creation care*. Grand Rapids, MI: Baker.

Brooks, D. (2015). *The Road to Character*. New York, NY: Random House.

Brown, B. (2012). *Daring Greatly: how the courage to be vulnerable transforms the way we live, love, parent and lead*. New York, NY: Avery.

Cain, S. (2012). *Quiet: the power of introverts in a world that just can't stop talking*. New York, NY: Random House.

Cairns, S. (2009). *The End of Suffering: Finding Purpose in Pain*. Brewster, MA: Paraclete Press.

Capon, R.F. (1982). *An Offering of Uncles: the Priesthood of Adam and the Shape of the World*. New York, NY: Crossroad Publishing.

Connolly, W. (1999). *Why I am Not a Secularist*. Minneapolis, MN: University of Minnesota Press.

Carroll, J. (2010). *The Wreck of Western Culture: Humanism Revisited*. Wilmington, DE: Intercollegiate Studies Institute.

Cloud, H. and J. Townsend (2008), *Boundaries: When to say Yes and when to say No*. Grand Rapids, MI: Zondervan Publishing

Coupland, D. (1994). *Life After God*. New York, NY: Simon & Schuster.

Crawford, M.B. (2015). *The World Beyond Your Head: on becoming an individual in an age of distractions*. New York, NY: Farrar, Straus and Giroux.

Craig, W.L. and C. Meister (eds.) (2009). *God is Great, God is Good: why believing in God is reasonable and responsible*. Downers Grove, IL: InterVarsity Press.

Crouch, A. (2008). *Culture Making: recovering our creative calling*. Downers Grove, IL: InterVarsity Press.

Crouch, A. (2013). *Playing God: redeeming the gift of power*. Downers Grove, IL: InterVarsity Press.

Dallaire, R. (2003). *Shake Hands with the Devil: the Failure of Humanity in Rwanda*. Toronto, ON: Random House Canada.

Dallmayr, F. (2010). *Integral Pluralism: beyond culture wars*. Lexington, KY: The University Press of Kentucky.

Downing, C.L. (2006). *How Postmodernism Serves (My) Faith: questioning truth in language, philosophy and art*. Downers Grove, IL: InterVarsity Press.

Eagleton, T. (1990). *The Ideology of the Aesthetic*. Oxford, UK: Blackwell.

Felten, P., H. D. L. Bauman, A. Kheriaty and E. Taylor (2013). *Transforming Conversations: a guide to mentoring communities among colleagues in higher education*. Hoboken, NJ: Wiley.

Ford, D.F. (1999). *Self and Salvation: Being transformed*. Cambridge, UK: Cambridge University Press.

Frankl, V. E. (2006). *Man's Search for Meaning*. Beacon Press.

Freeland, C. (2012). *Plutocrats: the rise of the new global super rich and the fall of everyone else*. Toronto, ON: Doubleday Canada.

Gawronski, R. (1995). *Word and Silence: Hans Urs Von Balthasar and the Spiritual Encounter Between East and West*. New York, NY: T & T Clarke

Gay, C.M. (1998). *The Way of the (Modern) World: or why it is tempting to live as if God doesn't exist*. Grand Rapids, MI: Eerdmans.

Girard, R. (1978). *Things Hidden Since the Foundation of the World*. Palo Alto, CA: Stanford University Press.

Girard, R. (2002). *I See Satan Fall Like Lightning*. Maryknoll, NY: Orbis Books.

Gore, A. (2013). *The Future: six drivers of global change*. New York, NY: Random House.

Greenway, W. (2000). "Charles Taylor on Affirmation, Mutilation, and Theism: A Retrospective Reading of Sources of the Self", *Journal of Religion, 80, No. 1* 23-40.

Greenleaf, R.K. (1998). *The Power of Servant Leadership*. San Francisco, CA: Berrett-Koehler Publishers, Inc.

Gregory, B. (2012). *The Unintended Reformation: how a religious revolution secularized society*. Cambridge, MA: Harvard University Press.

Habermas, J. (1986). *Taking Aim at the Heart of the Present*. In D.C. Hoy (Ed.) *Foucault: A critical reader*. Oxford, UK: Blackwell.

Habermas, J. (1987). *The Philosophical Discourse of Modernity*. Cambridge, UK: Polity Press.

Hare, J. (1996). *The Moral Gap: Kantian Ethics, Human Limits and God's Assistance*. Oxford, UK: Clarendon.

Harris, S. (2010). *The Moral Landscape: how science can determine human values*. New York, NY: Free Press

Harrison, P. (1998). *The Bible, Protestantism, and the Rise of Natural Science*. Cambridge, UK: Cambridge University Press.

Hart, D.B. (2009). *Atheist Delusions: the Christian revolution and its fashionable enemies*. New Haven, CT: Yale University Press.

Hart, D.B. (2013). *The Experience of God: being, consciousness, bliss*. New Haven, CT: Yale University Press.

Howard, T. (2011). *Chance or the Dance? A Critique of Modern Secularism*. San Francisco, CA: Ignatius Press.

Houston, J.M. (2006). *Joyful Exiles: life in Christ on the dangerous edge of things*. Downers Grove, IL: InterVarsity Press.

Houston, J.M. (2011). *The Mentored Life: From Individualism to Personhood.* Vancouver, B.C.: Regent College Publishing.

Hunter, J.D. (2010). *To Change the World: the Irony, Tragedy and Possibility of Christianity in the Late Modern World*. Oxford, UK: Oxford University Press.

Jackson, T. (2015). "Prophetic Conclusion: Martin Luther King Jr." In *Political Agape: Christian Love and Liberal Democracy* (381-408). Grand Rapid, MI: Eerdmans.

Johnson, P. (1983). *A History of the Modern World: from 1917 to the 1990s*. London, UK: Weidenfeld and Nicolson.

Keller, T. (2008). *Reason for God: Belief in an Age of Skepticism*. New York, NY: Riverhead Books.

Kreeft, P. (1986). *Making Sense Out of Suffering*. Cincinnati, OH: Franciscan Media.

Klein, N. (2014). *This Changes Everything: Capitalism versus the Climate.* New York, NY: Simon and Schuster.

Klein, S. (2002). *The Science of Happiness: how our brains make us happy – and what we can do to get happier*. Cambridge, MA: Da Capo Press.

Lewis, C. S. (1974) *The Four Loves.* London, UK: Collins.

Lundin, R. (1993). *Culture of Interpretation: Christian Faith and the Postmodern World.* Grand Rapids, MI: Eerdmans.

Loconte, J. (2015). *A Hobbit, a Wardrobe, and a Great War: How J.R.R. Tolkien and C.S. Lewis Rediscovered Faith, Friendship, and Heroism in the Cataclysm of 1914-18.* Nashville, TN: Thomas Nelson.

Long, D.S. (2001). *The Goodness of God*. Grand Rapids, MI: Brazos Press.

Long, D.S. (2009). *Speaking of God: Language, Theology and Truth.* Grand Rapids,MI: Eerdmans.

MacIntyre, A. (2007). *After Virtue: a study in moral theory* (3rd edition). Notre Dame, IN: University of Notre Dame Press.

MacIntyre, A. (1990). *Three Rival Versions of Moral Inquiry: Encyclopedia, Genealogy and Tradition.* Notre Dame, IN: University of Notre Dame Press

McFadyen, A.I. (1990). *The Call to Personhood: A Christian theory of the individual in social relationships.* Cambridge, UK: Cambridge University Press.

McFadyen, A.I. (1995). "Sins of Praise: the Assault on God's Freedom." In C. Gunton (Ed.). *God & Freedom: Essays in historical and systematic theology* (36-56). Edinburgh, UK: T. & T. Clark.

McGrath, A.E. (2009). *A Fine-Tuned Universe: the Quest for God in Science and Theology.* Louisville, KY: John Knox Press.

McLeish, T. (2014). *Faith and Wisdom in Science.* Oxford, UK: Oxford University Press.

McNay, L. (1992). *Foucault and Feminism: Power, Gender and the Self.* Cambridge, UK: Polity.

McNay, L. (1994). *Foucault: A Critical Reader*. Cambridge, UK: Polity.

Merton, T. (1961). *New Seeds of Contemplation*. New York, NY: New Directions.

Middleton, J.R. (2005). *The Liberating Image: The Imago Dei in Genesis 1.* Grand Rapids, MI: Brazos Press.

Morgan, M. (1994). "Religion, History and Moral Discourse." In J. Tully, (Ed.), *Philosophy in an Age of Pluralism: The Philosophy of Charles Taylor in Question*. Cambridge, UK: Cambridge University Press.

Moser, P.K. (2009). "Evidence of a Morally Perfect God." In W. L. Craig and C. Meister (Eds.) *God is Great, God is Good: why belief in God is reasonable and responsible*. Downers Grove, IL: InterVarsity Press.

Murdoch, I. (1997). "On 'God' and the 'Good'." In P. Conradi (Ed.) *Iris Murdoch on Existentialists and Mystics: Writings on Philosophy and Literature*. London, UK: Chatto & Windus.

Myers, J. (July 25, 2015). *Is it True that "The World Will be Saved by Beauty?"* First Things Journal.

Nagel, T. (2012). *Mind and Cosmos: Why the Materialist Neo-Darwinian Conception of Nature Is Almost Certainly False*. Oxford, UK: Oxford University Press.

Newbigin, L. (1986). *Foolishness to the Greeks: the Gospel and Western Culture*. Grand Rapids, MI: Eerdmans.

Nouwen, H. (2014). *Peacework: Prayer, Resistance, Community*. Ossining, NY: Orbis Books.

O'Leary, T. (2002). *Foucault and the Art of Ethics*. New York, NY: Continuum.

Page, D. (2009). *Servant-Empowered Leadership*. Langley, B.C.: Power to Change.

Palmer, P. J. (2004). *A Hidden Wholeness: the journey towards the undivided life*. San Francisco, CA: Jossey Bass Wiley.

Pasewark, K. (1993). *A Theology of Power: Being beyond domination*. Minneapolis, MN: Fortress Press.

Peck, M.S. MD. (1985). *People of the Lie: The Hope for Healing Human Evil*. New York, NY: Touchstone Books.

Peck, M.S. MD. (1978). *The Road Less Traveled: A New Psychology of Love, Traditional Values and Spiritual Growth*. New York, NY: Simon & Schuster.

Percy, W. (1983). *Lost in the Cosmos: the last great self-help book*. New York, NY: Farrar, Strauss and Giroux

Peterson, E. H. (2010). *Practice Resurrection: a conversation on growing up in Christ*. Grand Rapids, MI: Eerdmans.

Peterson, E. H. (2007). *The Jesus Way: a conversation on the ways that Jesus is the way*. Grand Rapids, MI: Eerdmans.

Pieper J. (1954). *The Four Cardinal Virtues: prudence, justice, fortitude, temperance*. Notre Dame, IN: University of Notre Dame Press.

Pippert, R. M. (2001). *Hope Has its Reasons: the search to satisfy our deepest longings*. Downers Grove, IL: InterVarsity Press

Plantinga, A. (2012). *Where the Conflict Really Lies: Science, Religion and Naturalism*. Oxford, UK: Oxford University Press.

Polanyi, M. (1958). *Personal Knowledge: Towards a Post-Critical Philosophy*. Chicago, IL: University of Chicago Press.

Richards, D.A. (2009) *God Is: my search for faith in a secular world*. Toronto, ON: Anchor Canada.

Ricoeur, P. (1992). *Oneself as Another*. Chicago, IL: University of Chicago Press.

Rifkin, J. (2014). *The Zero Marginal Cost Society: the internet of things, the collaborative commons and the eclipse of capitalism*. New York, NY: Palgrave MacMillan.

Russell, C.A. (1985). *Cross-currents: Interactions Between Science and Faith*. Downers Grove, IL: InterVarsity Press.

Sacks, J. (2002). *Dignity of Difference: how to avoid the clash of civilizations*. New York, NY: Continuum.

Schrag, C. (1997). *The Self After Postmodernity*. New Haven, CT: Yale University Press.

Schumacher, E.F. (1977). *A Guide for the Perplexed*. Preston, UK: Abacus Press.

Schwöbel, C. (1992). "God's Goodness and Human Morality." In C. Schwöbel, *God: Action and Revelation* (63-82). Kampen, Holland: Pharos.

Schwöbel, C. (1995). "Imago Libertatis: Human and Divine Freedom." In C. Gunton (Ed.) *God & Freedom: Essays in historical and systematic theology* (57-81). Edinburgh: T. & T. Clark.

Schultze, Q. J. (2002). *Habits of the High-Tech Heart*. Grand Rapids, MI: Baker Academic.

Sire, J.W. (2009). *The Universe Next Door: a Basic Worldview Catalogue*. Downers Grove, IL: InterVarsity Press.

Smith, C. & P. Snell (2009). *Souls in Transition: the religious and spiritual lives of emerging adults*. Oxford, UK: Oxford University Press.

Smith, J.K.A. (2014). *How (Not) to Be Secular: Reading Charles Taylor*. Grand Rapids, MI: Eerdmans

Smith, R. S. (2014). *In Search of Moral Knowledge: overcoming the fact-value dichotomy*. Downers Grove, IL: IVP Academic.

Soltes, E. (2016). *Why They Do It: Inside the Mind of the White-Collar Criminal*.

Solzhenitsyn, A. (2011). *Gulag Archipelago 1918-56*. New York, NY: Random House.

Sommerville, C. J. (2006). *The Decline of the Secular University*. Oxford, UK: Oxford University Press.

Steiner, G. (1991). *Real Presences: Is there anything in what we say?* Chicago, IL: University of Chicago Press.

Stiglitz, J.E. (2015). *The Great Divide: unequal societies and what can be done about them*. New York, NY: W.W. Norton.

Sullivan, R. (2015). *Stalin's Daughter: the extraordinary and tumultuous life of Svetlana Alliluyeva*. Toronto, ON: Harper Collins.

Taylor, C. (1989). *Sources of the Self: the making of the modern identity*. Cambridge, MA: Harvard University Press.

Taylor, C. (1991). *The Malaise of Modernity*. Concord, ON: Anansi.

Taylor, C. (1994). "Charles Taylor Replies." In J. Tully (Ed.) *Philosophy in an Age of Pluralism: The philosophy of Charles Taylor in question* (213-57). Cambridge, UK: Cambridge University Press.

Taylor, C. (1999). In J.L. Heft (S.M.). (Ed.). *A Catholic Modernity?* Oxford, UK: Oxford University Press.

Taylor, C. (2007). *A Secular Age*. Cambridge, MA: Harvard University Press.

Taylor, M. (2007). *After God (Religion and Postmodernism)*. Chicago, IL: University of Chicago Press.

Thistleton, A.C. (1995). *Interpreting God and the Postmodern Self: On meaning, manipulation and promise*. Edinburgh, UK: T. & T. Clark.

Thompson, C. (2010). *The Anatomy of the Soul: surprising connections between neuroscience and spiritual practices that can transform your life and relationships*. Carol Stream, IL: Tyndale House Publishers.

Thompson, C. (2015). *The Soul of Shame*. Downers Grove, IL: InterVarsity Press.

Tinder, G. (1991). *The Political Meaning of Christianity: The Prophetic Stance. An Interpretation*. Toronto, ON: Harper Collins

Turkle, S. (2015). *Reclaiming Conversation: the power of talk in a digital age*. London, UK: Penguin

Twenge, M. & N.K. Campbell (2009). *The Narcissistic Epidemic: Living in a Age of Entitlement.* New York, NY: Free Press.

Vanhoozer, K.J. (2009). *Is There a Meaning in This Text?: The Bible, the Reader, and the Morality of Literary Knowledge.* Grand Rapids, MI: Zondervan.

Vanier, J. (1999). *Becoming Human.* Toronto, ON: House of Anansi Press.

Volf, M. (1996). *Exclusion and Embrace: a theological exploration of identity, otherness and reconciliation.* Nashville, TN: Abingdon Press.

Volf, M. (2015). *Flourishing: why we need religion in a globalized world.* New Haven, CT: Yale University Press.

Voskamp, A. (2011). *One Thousand Gifts: a dare to live fully right where you are.* Grand Rapids, MI: Zondervan.

Wallis, J. (2014). *The (Un)Common Good: how the gospel brings hope to a world divided.* Grand Rapids, MI: Brazos.

Weber, C. (2013). *Surprised by Oxford: a memoir.* Nashville, TN: Thomas Nelson Publishers.

Williams, R. (2005). *The Truce of God: peacemaking in troubled times.* Grand Rapids, MI: Eerdmans.

Wong, P. T. P. (Ed.). (2012). *The human quest for meaning: Theories, research, and applications* (2nd Edition). New York, NY: Routledge.

Wright, N.T. (2011). *After You Believe: why Christian character matters.* Toronto, ON: Harper One.

Yancey, P. (2000). *Reaching for the Invisible God.* Grand Rapids, MI: Zondervan.

Zagzebski, L. T. (1996). *Virtues of the Mind: An Inquiry into the Nature of Virtue and the Ethical Foundations of Knowledge.* Cambridge, UK: Cambridge University Press.

Zimmermann, J. (2012a). *Incarnational Humanism: a philosophy of culture for the church in the world.* Downers Grove, IL: IVP Academic.

Zimmermann, J. (2012b). *Humanism and Religion: a call for the renewal of western culture.* Oxford, UK: Oxford University Press.

Zimmermann, J. & N. Klassen (2006). *The Passionate Intellect: incarnational humanism and the future of the university.* Grand Rapids, MI: Baker Academic.

Zimmermann, J. (2015). *Hermeneutics: a very short introduction.* Oxford, UK: Oxford University Press.

40805357R00137

Made in the USA
Middletown, DE
24 February 2017